W9-AHT-933

DORLING KINDERSLEY DK EYEWITNESS BOOKS

SOCCER

DON DU PETROLE HAHN POUR LES CHEVEUX

GRAND MATCH D'ASSOCIATION

1930s French hair-oil advertisement

1905 match holder

1900s ball pumps

1900s shin pads

1910s shin pads

1930s shin pads

Jay Jay Okacha of Nigeria

Early 20th-century soccer stencils

1966 World Cup soccer ball

1998 World Cup soccer ball

1930s painting of a goalkeeper

Porcelain figure

Porcelain figure

DK EYEWITNESS BOOKS

SOCCER

Written by
HUGH HORNBY

Photographed by
ANDY CRAWFORD

1912 soccer ball

Dorling Kindersley

19th-century jersey

1925 Australian International shirt

1905 book cover image

1900s plaster figure

1908 Newcastle shirt

DK

Dorling Kindersley
LONDON, NEW YORK, DELHI, JOHANNESBURG, MUNICH, PARIS and SYDNEY

For a full catalog, visit

DK www.dk.com

Project editor Louise Pritchard
Art editor Jill Plank
Assistant editor Annabel Blackledge
Assistant art editor Yolanda Belton
US editor Irene Pavitt
Managing editor Sue Grabham
Senior managing art editor Julia Harris
Production Kate Oliver
Picture research Amanda Gregory
DTP designers Andrew O'Brien and Georgia Bryer

This Eyewitness ® Book has been conceived by
Dorling Kindersley Limited and Editions Gallimard

Published in the United States by
Dorling Kindersley Publishing, Inc.
95 Madison Avenue
New York, NY 10016
2 4 6 8 10 9 7 5 3 1

Dorling Kindersley books are available at special discounts for bulk purchases for sales promotions or premiums. Special editions, including personalized covers, excerpts of existing guides, and corporate imprints can be created in large quantities for specific needs. For more information, contact Special Markets Dept., Dorling Kindersley Publishing, Inc., 95 Madison Ave., New York, NY 10016; Fax: (800) 600-9098

Library of Congress Cataloging-in-Publication Data
Hornby, Hugh.
Soccer / written by Hugh Hornby. — 1st American ed.
p. cm. — (Eyewitness Books)
Includes index.
Summary: Examines all aspects of the game of soccer: its history, rules, techniques, tactics, equipment, playing fields, competitive play, and more.
1. Soccer—Juvenile literature. [1. Soccer.] I. Title. II. Series.
GV943.25. H67 2000 796.334—dc21
ISBN 0-7894-6284-2 (pb)
ISBN 0-7894-5245-6 (hc)

Color reproduction by Colourscan, Singapore
Printed in China by Toppan Printing Co. (Shenzhen) Ltd.

1905 book cover image

1940s whistle

THE REFEREE

Early 20th-century snap card

1895 penknife

SUNDERLAND

1900 penknife

1930s silver hat pin

1900s silver match holder

1920s silver flint lighter

Shirts from 1890s catalog

Contents

Hungary patch   Holland patch   Italy patch   Brazil patch

8
The global game
10
History of soccer
12
Rules of the game
14
The referee
16
The field
18
Soccer skills
20
The goalkeeper
22
Tactics
24
Injury time
26
Soccer balls
28
Soccer shoes
30
Soccer uniforms
32
Accessories
34
Famous players
38
Medals and caps
40
Famous teams

42
The fans
44
Game day
46
The stadium
48
The World Cup
52
Cups and trophies
54
Playing the game
56
Memorabilia
58
The business of soccer
60
Index

1940s air-raid patrolman's rattle

1900 adult's rattle

Early 20th-century child's rattle

1930s child's painted rattle

1940s air-raid patrolman's bell

The global game

SOCCER HAS ITS ROOTS IN ancient China, Europe, and the Americas. People kicked a ball to prepare for war, to honor their gods, or just to entertain themselves. For centuries, different versions of ball-kicking games existed. In Europe, they were tests of courage and strength; in China and other Eastern countries, the games were rituals of grace and skill. The rules of the modern game of soccer were not drawn up until 1863, but the qualities that we admire in it – speed, agility, bravery, and spirit – have been present in many cultures for more than 2,000 years.

An Ashbourne ball

ASHBOURNE BALL
Ashbourne in Derbyshire, England, is the site of one of several traditional Shrove Tuesday soccer games. It is characterized by disorder. Two teams, the Upwards and the Downwards, try to move the ball through the opposition's "goal" – a gateway at the other end of town.

HARROW BALL
English private schools, including Harrow and Eton, played a crucial role in developing modern soccer in the early 1800s. Although the schools played the game differently, they all produced detailed, written rules. These provided the basis for the first official rules.

The Harrow ball was flattened, top and bottom.

SOCCER TRAINING
The Chinese were playing a type of soccer as long ago as the third century BC. A military book of that period refers to *tsu chu*, or "kicking a ball." The game may once have been part of a soldier's training and was later included in ceremonies on the emperor's birthday.

These symbols were once described by an official of the English Football Association as "To kick with the foot."

Chinese characters meaning "football"

A GENTLEMEN'S GAME
The game of calcio was played in Italian cities such as Venice and Florence in the 16th and 17th centuries. On certain festival days, two teams of gentlemen would attempt to force the ball through openings at either end of a city square. Although physical contact was a feature of calcio, the game also had a tactical element. Teams used formations and attempted to create space in which to advance.

Local people came out to watch the games.

Handling the ball was part of the game.

Players have to wear an elaborate costume of silk and gold brocade.

Ball made from strips of leather

Men from many different backgrounds played soccer.

STREET GAMES
This early 19th century cartoon is subtitled "Dustmen, coalmen, gentlemen, and city clerks at murderous if democratic play." It shows the violent "every man for himself" spirit common to street games in Britain at that time. The damage done to property, particularly windows, and the disruption to the lives of other citizens caused many town councils to ban soccer – without much success.

ANCIENT RITUAL
The Japanese game of kemari probably developed in the 7th century from an ancient Chinese football game, after contact was made between the two countries. In contrast to the chaotic early soccer brawls of Europe, it involved many rituals and was played as part of a ceremony. The game is still played and involves keeping the ball in the air inside a small court.

Kemari is a game of balance and skill.

FOOTBALL WRITING
Football has been a popular literary subject for as long as the game has been played. The first known book devoted to soccer is *Discourse on calcio* by Giovanni da Bardi, published in 1580 in Florence, Italy. Soccer has inspired poetry too. "A Match at Football" by Matthew Concanen was published in an anthology in the 18th century. The popularity of soccer increased rapidly in the early 20th century. *The School Across the Road* by Desmond Coke is one of many children's books published at around that time.

16th-century discourse on soccer

18th-century anthology

The children's book The School Across the Road

Color plates appear throughout the book

Image from a 19th-century watercolor on silk

History of soccer

THE GAME THAT HAS CAPTURED the imagination of people all over the world was developed in England and Scotland in the 19th century. Graduates of English private schools produced the first common set of rules and formed the Football Association (FA) in 1863. Things moved forward quickly. British administrators, merchants, and engineers took the game overseas, and people from other countries began to play soccer. The first International matches were followed by professional leagues and big competitions.

Lord Kinnaird once did a headstand after winning a Cup final.

CELEBRITY PLAYER
The first soccer players were amateurs. C.B. Fry, who played for the Corinthians in the late 1890s, was one of the first soccer celebrities. He was also a member of the England cricket team and held the world long-jump record.

Arnold Kirke Smith's cap

EXHIBITIONISM
Throughout the early years of the 20th century, British teams toured the world, introducing soccer to other countries by playing exhibition matches. This shield was presented to the Islington Corinthians in Japan, in 1937.

The English Three Lions motif was first used in 1872.

Arnold Kirke Smith's England shirt

The shirt is made of closely woven wool.

THE FIRST INTERNATIONAL
In November 1872, Scotland played England on a cricket field in Glasgow in the first International match. About 2,000 spectators watched a 0–0 draw. This shirt and cap were worn by Arnold Kirke Smith from Oxford University, who was a member of the England team.

MODERN RULES
Lord Kinnaird was president of the Football Association from 1890–1923, and was one of the amateurs who shaped the rules and structure of the modern game. Previously, he had played in nine of the first 12 FA Cup finals, winning five.

TALENTED TEAMS
The English Football League began in 1888. Its 12-team fixture program was inspired by baseball. This picture by Thomas Hemy shows two successful English clubs of the 1890s: Aston Villa which won the league five times, and Sunderland, "the team of all talents," which won three times.

THE UNRULY GAME

The first French soccer league, set up in 1894, was dominated by teams of Scottish emigrants, such as the White Rovers and Standard AC. French satirists were quick to refer to the game's reputation for unruliness. This 1900s French magazine, *Le Monde comique*, reflects this attitude toward the game.

In reality, women's uniforms were far less figure hugging.

A ball of exaggerated size

Bystanders often got caught up in the boisterous action.

Cover illustration entitled *Les Plaisirs du dimanche* (Sunday Pleasures)

LADIES FIRST

Women's soccer started at the end of the 19th century. Teams such as the British Ladies' Club attracted large crowds. During World War I, men's and women's teams played against each other for charity. The first women's World Cup was held in China in 1991 and was won by the US.

FIFA patch

FORMING FIFA

By 1904, several countries, including France, Belgium, Denmark, the Netherlands, Spain, Sweden, and Switzerland, had their own administrators. They formed the world governing body, FIFA (Fédération Internationale de Football Associations). By 1939, more than 50 countries had joined.

This 1900s plaster figure is wearing shin pads that were typical of that time.

Ugandan batik

Each stamp shows a different US player.

US stamps produced for the 1994 World Cup

OUT OF AFRICA

Soccer spread through Africa from both ends of the continent. South Africa, with its European populations, was an obvious foothold and sent a touring party to South America in 1906. In 1923, Egypt, in North Africa, was the first African team to join FIFA.

AMERICAN SOCCER

Youth soccer is the most widely played sport in the US, for both boys and girls. The 1994 World Cup provided a big boost for Major League Soccer, which is bringing top-level professional games to a new audience. The US reached the semifinals of the very first World Cup in 1930.

Rules of the game

THE RULES OF A GAME should be brief and easy to understand. It is certain that soccer's success has been partly due to the simplicity of its rules. Rules governing equipment, the field, foul play, and restarts have all survived the passage of time. Soccer has always been a free-flowing game. Stoppages can be avoided if the referee uses the advantage rule – allowing play to continue after a foul, providing that the right team still has the ball. The offside rule has always been a source of controversy in the game. The assistant referees have to make split-second decisions about whether an attacker has strayed beyond the second last defender at the moment the ball is played forward by one of his or her team-mates. A player cannot be offside from a throw-in.

STAND BACK
This throw-in is illegal. The ball is held correctly in both hands, but the feet, though they are both on the ground as they should be, are over the line.

There have been goalposts since the early days of soccer but, until the crossbar was introduced in 1875, tape was stretched between them 8 ft (2.5 m) from the ground.

The penalty spot is 12 yd (11 m) from the goal line.

Goal kicks must be taken from within the 6-yd (5.5-m) box.

Players must not cross the half-way line until the ball is kicked off.

PENALTY
Penalties were introduced in 1891 as a punishment for foul play, such as tripping, pushing, or handball in the 18-yd (16.5-m) box. A player takes a shot at goal from the penalty spot with only the goalkeeper to beat. If the ball rebounds from the post or bar, the penalty taker cannot play it again before someone else has touched it.

FREE KICK
There are two types of free kick – direct and indirect. In an indirect free kick, awarded after an infringement of a rule, the ball must be touched by two players before a goal is scored. Direct free kicks are given after fouls, and the taker may score immediately. Opposing players must be at least 10 yd (9 m) away from the ball at a free kick.

CORNER
A corner kick is taken when the defending team puts the ball out of play behind their own goal-line. Corner kicks provide useful goal-scoring opportunities. The ball must be placed within the quadrant – a quarter circle with a radius of 1 yd (1 m) in the corner of the field. A goal can be scored directly from a corner kick.

FAKING FOULS
The amateur soccer players of the 19th century believed that all fouls were accidental and would have been horrified by the "professional foul," an offense deliberately committed to prevent an attack from developing. The game today is full of deliberate fouls. Some players also fake being fouled to win their team a free kick.

When a penalty is taken, only the taker is allowed inside the "D."

CHARGE!
The 1958 English FA Cup final between Manchester United and Bolton Wanderers is remembered for the disputed goal scored by Bolton's center-forward, Nat Lofthouse. He charged the United goalkeeper, Harry Gregg, over the line as he caught the ball – a challenge that all referees today would consider a foul.

Players from the defending team must stay out of the 10-yd (9-m) circle before the kickoff.

Players cannot be offside in their own half of the field.

The 6-yd (5.5-m) and 18-yd (16.5-m) boxes were semicircular until 1902.

"STANL
Stanley matthews
REGD NO 733.94-7

A goalkeeper is restricted to four steps when kicking a ball out of the hands.

Assistant referees patrol opposite sides of the field and cover one-half each, their main responsibilities being to signal throw-ins and flag for offside.

PERMANENT MARKERS
In the mid 19th century, before it was stipulated that permanent lines should be marked on the field, flags were used as a guide to whether the ball was out of play. Today, a corner flag has to be at least 5 ft (1.5 m) high to avoid the risk of players being impaled.

LAW AND ORDER
There are 17 main soccer rules. The field of play must be rectangular and, for a full-size field, from 110 to 120 yd (100.5 to 110 m) long and from 70 to 80 yd (64 to 73 m) wide. There should be 11 players per side. Substitution rules have changed over the years, and teams may now substitute any three from five players, including the goalie, during stoppages in the match. The duration of play is 90 minutes, in two halves of 45 minutes each.

Goal nets were first manufactured by Brodies of Liverpool, England, in 1891 and welcomed as a means of settling disputes about whether a ball had actually entered the goal.

13

The referee

THE REFEREE

Early 20th century caricature of a referee on a card for the game snap.

EﾄﾃARLY AMATEUR players put a high value on fair play, but saw the need for officials on the soccer field. To begin with, each team provided an umpire from their own club, who didn't interfere much with the passage of play. At this stage, players had to raise an arm and appeal for a decision if they felt that they had been fouled; otherwise, play continued. The rise of professional football in the 1880s made it harder for umpires to be neutral. A referee was introduced to settle disputes. In 1891, the referee was moved on to the field of play and the umpires became linesmen, a system that has continued ever since. Linesmen and women, are now called assistant referees.

YOUR NUMBER'S UP
One duty of the assistant referees is to control the entrance of substitutes to the field, checking their cleats and indicating with number cards which player is to be replaced. At top levels of the game, a fourth official uses an illuminated board to indicate substitutes and inform everyone how much injury time will be played at the end of each half.

CLASSIC BLACK
This is the classic referee's uniform, all black with white cuffs and collar. Dating from the 1970s, it is similar to all those worn from the phasing out of the blazer in the 1940s to the introduction of other colors in the 1990s. The bulky jackets of the early 1900s were replaced by a less constricting shirt to encourage the officials to keep up with play on the field.

White trim sets off the all-black uniform

Notebook to record bookings, goals, expulsions, and substitutions

The yellow card is shown for bookable offenses.

WORKSOP

Patch refers to the referee's local association.

Serious foul play results in a red card and expulsion.

1940s Acme whistle

Referees must look professional, with shirt tucked in at all times.

Both sides of a FIFA Fair Play coin

TOOLS OF THE TRADE
Certain items are vital to the referee's job. Red and yellow cards may seem like a long-established part of soccer, but they were introduced only in the 1970s. The whistle was first used in 1878 and was soon recognized as the best way of controlling play. Barrel-shaped whistles used to predominate, but other shapes are now common. The referee carries a notebook and pencil to record details of the game and a special coin that is tossed to decide which team kicks off and in which direction.

Referees may carry a handkerchief in case players get dirt in their eyes.

YOU'RE CARDED

Cards used to be given only once or twice per match, and expulsions were extremely rare, but FIFA now insists that referees be much stricter. As a result, teams regularly have to play with 10 team members or even fewer.

Former USSR

Australia

New Zealand

Bangladesh

Iceland

Portugal

USA

Columbia

Italy

Cards are produced with a flourish from this pocket

The referee times the game with a watch.

The referee has to be fit to keep up with play on the field.

WORLD-CLASS REFEREES

These badges are produced by Referees' Associations around the world. Despite all the abuse they receive, referees are motivated by the prospect of officiating at top-class games. World Cup matches are controlled by officials from all countries affiliated with FIFA, not just those that qualify as competitors.

LINESMAN FIFA 92

LINESWOMAN FIFA 95

Official FIFA patches for sewing on the officials' shirts

Men and women officiate at top-level soccer games.

TOUCHLINE HELPERS

The first linesmen waved a handkerchief to alert the referee. Assistant referees today use a flag. They wave the flag when a player is offside, when the ball is out of play, and when they have seen an infringement on the field.

Blazer with pockets for a stopwatch and notebook

The first referees wore plus-two trousers.

HOW TO BE A REFEREE

This illustration from the cover of a 1906 book entitled *How to Be a Referee* shows the typical referee's clothing of that period. After taking a qualifying exam, referees usually start out at amateur level. They are assessed regularly to ensure that standards remain high. Eventually, after years of experience, referees may progress to officiate at international tournaments.

The field

This Samuel Brandão painting of Rio de Janeiro shows football being played on bare earth.

AT THE START OF A SEASON, soccer players can look forward to playing their first game on a smooth green field. If a field is not looked after, it soon becomes muddy and uneven, especially if cold, wet weather sets in. Groundskeepers try to keep the fields in good condition with the help of new species of grass and good drainage. In many northern European countries, soccer takes a midwinter break during the worst conditions. Wealthy teams may lay completely new turf between matches, but millions of amateur players have to make do with whatever muddy or frozen land is available.

Patterns can be made when mowing the field

STREETS AHEAD
In the days before traffic became too heavy, street soccer was a popular pastime. Children learned close ball control and dribbling skills in confined spaces. They often used heaps of clothes or gateways as goalposts.

Jean-Pierre Papin playing for AC Milan, Italy, on a snow-covered field

Groundskeepers preparing for a match during the 1953 English season

PLAYING IN SNOW
In snowy weather, the field markings and the white soccer ball are hard to see and the ground is slippery. If the markings can be swept clear and the field is soft enough to take a cleat, soccer usually can be played, using a more visible orange ball.

HOT STUFF
In countries where the weather is cold during the soccer season, many methods have been tried to prevent fields from freezing. Underground heating was first installed in England at Everton in 1958. Before underground heating became common, groundskeepers put straw down as insulation and lit fires in braziers to raise the air temperature. Today, large covers are sometimes used to protect fields.

SLOPES AND SHADE
Modern fields are usually laid with a camber, which means that they slope slightly down from the center circle to the touchlines. This helps drain water away. When large stands are built, less air and light reach the grass, stunting its growth. This has been a problem at some stadiums, such as the San Siro in Milan, Italy.

Grass is kept long to encourage deep rooting.

Layer of topsoil nourishes the grass.

Heating pipes laid in grids.

Layers of sand and gravel allow water to filter away.

PAMPERING THE FIELD
Modern field maintenance is a full-time job. In the summer, the grass must be mowed, watered, and fed regularly. During the close season, work is done to repair holes and worn patches in the turf. New types of grass have been developed that grow better in the shade of tall stands. This is vital in helping the groundskeepers to keep the field in good condition.

The surface is made to mimic grass.

Fibers are woven together to form a carpet.

Artificial grass viewed from the side, top, and underneath

The base of the field is composed of large pieces of stone.

Drainage pipes carry water away.

Model of a section through a field

BETTER THAN THE REAL THING?
Some fields are made from synthetic turf laid on a shock-absorbent pad. They are more hard-wearing than grass fields and are unaffected by torrential rain or freezing cold. A team with a field of artificial grass can rent out its stadium for a range of events, such as pop concerts, and its home matches need never be postponed because of bad weather. Many players do not like the surface because they feel that it increases the risk of injury.

SATURATION POINT
Rainwater is the greatest threat to field condition. Good built-in drainage is therefore an important part of field construction. Pipes and materials chosen for their good draining qualities are laid under he grass. A large amount of sand is mixed into the topsoil to make it less absorbent and less prone to becoming waterlogged. Even a well-maintained field may become saturated. Groundskeepers sometimes have to use garden forks to remove standing water.

Soccer skills

Early 20th century button showing a man heading the ball

EACH POSITION ON THE FIELD is associated with a specific range of tasks. Defenders must be able to tackle the opposition and claim the ball, midfielders need to pass the ball accurately to their teammates, and strikers have to shoot and score goals. Although most players specialize in a certain position, professional players are expected to master a range of skills and work on any weaknesses. As part of their daily training routine, they practice hard to perfect their skills so that their technique does not let them down in a game.

CONTROL FREAK

Some of the most gifted players, such as Brazil's Roberto Carlos, are able to manipulate the ball with their feet, making it swerve, curl, or dip. This type of ball control helps them bend passes around defenders and score from free-kicks well outside the penalty area.

Shouting helps the players pick one another out.

TACKLE TALK

Players try to take the ball from another player by tackling. Lilian Thuram of France and Parma, Italy, is one of the world's great tacklers. He shows the timing and precision that are essential to avoid committing a foul. Referees punish players if they make a physical challenge from behind or if they make contact with a player instead of the ball.

Lilian Thuram

Hand signals are used to improve teamwork.

PASS MARK

Moving the ball quickly around the pitch, from one player to another, is the most effective means of stretching a defence. Accurate passing remains the hallmark of all successful teams. Zinedine Zidane was the star of the 1998 World Cup final for France. He has the vision to pass the ball into space for his strikers even when he is tightly marked.

Constant movement into space is essential.

If the defender is unable to reach the ball, he must still challenge the striker.

The player must time his leap to meet the ball firmly.

Oliver Bierhoff

All parts of the foot are used to manipulate the ball in the desired direction

One-touch passing of the ball is the hardest to defend.

HEADS UP!

There are two distinct kinds of heading – defensive and attacking. Defenders try to gain distance when they clear a high ball out of the goal area. Attackers need accuracy and power to score goals with a header. Oliver Bierhoff of Germany, and Milan, Italy, is one of the best modern strikers in the air.

The ability to pass with both feet gives the player more options.

Leaning back helps to ensure that the ball will rise towards the top of the net.

GOING FOR GOAL
When shooting, forwards need the accuracy to find the corner of the net as well as the power to blast the ball through the defense. Gabriel Batistuta of Argentina beats goalkeepers regularly with his powerful right foot.

Keeping the head still improves accuracy.

Keeping your weight over the ball makes it easier to cross with power.

Extending the arms assists with balance.

WINGING IT
Crosses, or passes in from the wings, result in more goals than any other angle of attack. Players who can put the ball over with pace and accuracy are extremely valuable to a team. David Beckham of Manchester United and England is renowned for the way he crosses from the right wing, curling the ball around the fullback and away from the goalkeeper. This type of swinging cross is often used when players are taking corners. They curl the ball in from the corner toward the goal and the waiting strikers.

The left leg is firmly planted to allow the body to make the best shape for the cross.

The player can feint to go in one direction before going in the other.

The foot turns in as it passes through the ball to make it swerve.

The bicycle kick is even harder if the ball is moving across the player.

BICYCLE KICK
The bicycle kick was first demonstrated in the 1930s by Brazilian forward Leonidas. It is one of the most difficult skills to pull off. With their back to the goal, strikers throw their legs up in the air and kick the ball while falling backward. This tactic sometimes catches the goalkeeper by surprise. This model of Italian striker Roberto Baggio shows the ideal body position.

A higher jump allows the player to keep the ball down below the crossbar.

DOWNTOWN DRIBBLER
When a player runs with the ball at his feet, it is called dribbling. Brazilian star Ronaldo, who learned to play soccer on the streets of Rio de Janeiro, is proof that dribbling can cause problems for the opposition. Good balance and concentration help a dribbler change direction quickly and ride tackles.

The goalkeeper

A 1900s Vesta, or match holder, showing a goalkeeper punching clear

As THE LAST LINE of defense, a goalkeeper knows that a single mistake can cost the team victory. Goalkeeping can be a lonely job, requiring skills different from the rest of the team and sometimes involving several minutes of inactivity. The recent change in the back-pass law, forcing the goalkeeper to kick clear rather than pick up the ball, has made the job even harder. The necessity of having both a physical presence and great agility means that the goalkeeper has to train harder than any other player, but the reward for this diligence can be a much longer career than that of players in other positions.

Clothes

Until 1913, goalkeepers were distinguishable only by their cap, making it difficult for the referee to judge who, in a goalmouth scramble, was handling the ball. From 1913 to the early 1990s, they wore a shirt of a single plain color that was different from the shirts worn by the rest of their team. A rule that prohibited them from wearing short sleeves has now been relaxed.

GOOD SAVE
This 1950 comic cover shows the save that is considered to be the easiest to make – from a shot straight to the midriff. It also hints at the spectacular action in which goalkeepers are regularly involved, such as when they have to fly through the air to tip the ball away. Modern strikers are likely to make the ball swerve suddenly, so it is all the more important for goalies to keep their bodies in line with the ball.

CATCH IT
Punching the ball away from the danger area has always been popular among European and South American goalkeepers. The goalkeeper depicted on this 1900 book cover is trying to punch the ball, but he probably should be trying to catch it because he is not being closely challenged. In the modern game, referees rarely allow goalkeepers to be charged when they are attempting to catch the ball.

The ball should be punched out toward the wing.

KEEPERS' COLORS
Patterns in soccer shirts have traditionally been limited to stripes and rings, but since the rules on goalkeepers' clothes were relaxed, every combination of colors seems to have been tried. Not all of them have been easy on the eye, although fluorescent designs are easy for defenders to see.

Flexible plastic ribs reinforce each finger

Modern gloves help to prevent injuries such as a broken finger.

The shamrock, symbol of Ireland

EIRE SHIRT
This shirt was worn by Alan Kelly for the Republic of Ireland. He made 47 appearances, the first against West Germany in 1957 and the last against Norway in 1973. Yellow shirts were once a common sight in international matches. Green was not an option for the Irish goalkeeper because the strip of the Irish team is green.

GOALIE'S GLOVES
Until the 1970s, gloves were worn only when it was wet, and they were made of thin cotton. Modern goalkeepers wear gloves in all conditions. Various coatings and pads are used to increase the gloves' grip, which is the key to handling the ball.

NARROWING THE ANGLE
This image from the 1930s shows a goalkeeper alert to danger. When an attacker approaches the goal with the ball, goalkeepers should leave their line and move toward the ball to reduce the target area for the attacker. This "narrowing of the angle" is an important part of keepers' roles. They often make marks, in line with the posts, to help them keep their bearings when leaving the line.

Most goalkeepers may still wear a cap if the sun is in their eyes.

Arms are outstretched, ready to block a shot

THROWING OUT
This painted button from the 1900s shows one of the goalkeeper's jobs. A quick throw out, particularly after catching a corner, can be a way of launching an attack. Some goalkeepers are renowned for the length of their throw.

GOAL KICK
When the ball is put out behind the goal line by an attacker, the opposing team is awarded a goal kick. As shown on this button, the goalkeeper takes the kick from inside the 6-yard (5.5-m) box. When the ball was made of heavy leather, a goal kick rarely reached the opposition's half.

LOUD AND CLEAR
Peter Schmeichel is famous for the vehemence of his reaction when a teammate makes a mistake. Here he is shouting at Roy Keane when playing for Manchester United, England. Although such eruptions risk undermining team spirit, it is far better for goalkeepers to communicate with their defenders than to be quiet. Goalies also have to shout when organizing the wall at free kicks.

Tactics

Old Arabic print of team formations

Part of soccer's appeal is its tactical element. Coaches and managers try to outwit the opposition by keeping their tactics secret until the game. Since soccer first began, teams have lined up in different formations, trying to play in a way that will take their opponents by surprise and result in a goal. Early players had the physical attributes and skills needed for a particular position on the field. Today, the pace of the game demands that players be adaptable enough to play in almost any position, in the manner of the Dutch "total football" teams of the 1970s.

Center-half defended and attacked

2-3-5 formation (left)

Center-half only defended

W-M formation (right)

France won the 1998 World Cup with a back four.

Wingers have been replaced by midfielders who can also defend.

4-4-2 formation (right)

One forward often plays "in the hole" behind the other.

Wing-backs are responsible for providing attacking width.

Sweeper must be creative and pass accurately.

Sweeper system (left)

IN GOOD FORM (ABOVE)
The 2-3-5 formation dominated tactics until the 1930s. Each player had a very specific place and role on the field. Herbert Chapman of Arsenal, England, was the first manager to make a radical change, positioning the center-half and inside-forwards deeper to create the W-M formation.

GAME PLAN (ABOVE)
Managers use a board like this in the locker room. They employ it to show players how to counteract the opposition and where they should be at certain points in the game. This is particularly important when defending corners and free kicks.

CLEAN SWEEP
Modern formations are varied, but the 4-4-2 is one of the most popular. The four defenders are not expected to push forward and the four midfielders sometimes switch to a diamond shape. The sweeper system, perfected by the Italians in the 1960s, frees one player from marking duties to act as cover.

The forward cannot go "one on one" with the goalkeeper.

OFFSIDE ORIGINS

The first offside law stated that three defenders, including the goalkeeper, had to be between the attacker and the goal when the ball was being played forward by a team-mate. By 1920, fewer and fewer goals were being scored because, even if attackers were onside at the vital point, they still had to beat the last outfield defender.

OFFSIDE UPDATED

In 1925, FIFA decided to amend the offside law so that only two players had to be between the attacker and the goal. Immediately, far more goals were scored. The offside rule is basically unchanged today. Here, the midfielder is about to pass the ball to the forward. This player is still onside and, once in possession of the ball, will have only the goalkeeper to beat.

Player is offside.

OFFSIDE TRAP

Teams without a sweeper, like Norway under Egil Olsen, are still able to use an offside trap. As the midfielder prepares to pass the ball forward, the defenders suddenly advance up the field in a line, leaving the forward offside when the ball is played. William McCracken of Newcastle, England, was famous for first perfecting this tactic, in the years before World War One.

PACKED DEFENSE

Denial of space to the opposing forwards is vital, and certain players may be singled out for man-to-man coverage. It is often said that the best teams are built from the back, with a strong defense providing a springboard for attack. Here, several defenders are surrounding a striker.

The attacker is trapped.

The defenders are physically blocking in the attacker.

NO SUBSTITUTE

Substitutions were first allowed by FIFA in 1923, but only if a player was injured. Injuries were faked so often to let coaches make tactical changes that it was gradually accepted that one player could be freely replaced. Now the number of substitutions allowed per team has increased to five for some games.

BE PREPARED

Javier Zanetti's goal for Argentina against England at France '98 was an example of how a well-rehearsed routine can work brilliantly. Lots of goals are scored from set pieces – movements that a team practices before a game. Coaches spend a great deal of time going through these with the team during training.

Injury time

Mr Black the footballer from a Happy Families game

A PROFESSIONAL SOCCER PLAYER'S job involves far more than playing games and enjoying the limelight. Training, fitness, and recovery from injuries are day-to-day concerns for the modern player. Advances in medicine mean that injuries that a few years ago would have led to inevitable retirement, can now be successfully treated. The pace of the modern game is unrelenting, and loss of fitness is likely to stop a player from staying at the top level. Physiotherapy, nutrition, and even psychology are all parts of the conditioning program of big teams today.

FIGHTING FIT
Medicine balls like this were used in soccer training for many decades. They are extremely heavy, so throwing them improves stamina and builds muscle bulk. Sophisticated gym equipment, training programs, and resistance machines are now commonly used. Strength and fitness are essential to success in the modern game because top players have to play as many as 70 games per season. The greatest players are superb athletes as much as they are skilled soccer players.

VITAL EDGE
Vittorio Pozzo, one of the first great managers, led Italy to victory in the World Cup in 1934 and 1938. He realized the importance of physical fitness and made his team train hard to give it a vital edge over its opponents. This paid off in extra time in the 1934 final, when Italy eventually scored the winning goal.

WARM UP AND COOL DOWN
A proper game-day routine can help prolong a player's soccer career. Modern players are aware of the importance of warming up thoroughly before a game. The risk of muscle tears and strains is significantly reduced if the muscles are warm and loose. Recovery after games is also important. Many players "warm down" after a match to relax their muscles before resting them.

The stretcher is carried by two wooden poles.

GETTING CARRIED AWAY
This stretcher was used in the 1920s. In those days, if the stretcher was brought out on the field, the crowd knew that a player was seriously injured. Today, players are given a few moments to get up before they are carried off to prevent wasting time and delaying the game. They often resume shortly afterward. In the US, motorized buggies or carts have taken the place of traditional stretchers.

A pillow is built into the stretcher.

A piece of canvas supports the injured player.

AS IF BY MAGIC
The "magic" sponge has a special place in soccer folklore. Spectators have often wondered how a rubdown with a sponge and cold water could result in a player's swift recovery from an injury. Today, the team physiotherapist, rather than the trainer, treats players for injury problems on and off the field. Physiotherapists are fully qualified to give sophisticated treatment to injured players.

The sponge is still used in amateur games.

The physiotherapist carries equipment onto the field.

Physiotherapist's security pass

Modern medicine cases are light and waterproof

SOLDIERING ON
Injured players are usually substituted to prevent further harm, but some injuries do not need to stop a player from turning out for an important match. Paul Gascoigne, above, wore a plastic mask when playing for England against Poland in 1993, to protect a fractured cheekbone. During the 1978 World Cup final, Holland's Rene van der Kerkhof wore a cast on his hand.

FIELD DOCTOR
Nigeria's Daniel Amokachi is shown here being treated for a hamstring injury during a 1994 World Cup match. The hamstring muscle, at the back of the leg, is one of the most vulnerable for a player, and straining it usually results in a three- to four-week layoff.

Ice is applied to the injury to reduce inflammation.

The bag is made of leather.

LOTIONS AND POTIONS
This medicine bag belonged to Ramsgate FC in the early 20th century. It was a non-League team from Kent in England. The bottles would have contained various lotions and medicines to warm muscles, pour on grazes, or reduce pain. Professional teams in many countries are now required to have a doctor on hand at every game to deal with serious head injuries and fractures.

The trainer's medicines sometimes included chloroform, to sedate a badly injured player.

Soccer balls

An 1890s brass traveling inkwell in the shape of a soccer ball

Much of the appeal of soccer lies in the fact that it can be played without special equipment. Children everywhere know that a tin can, some bound-up rags, or a ball from a different sport entirely can be satisfyingly kicked around. This ingenuity was first displayed hundreds of years ago when people discovered that an animal's bladder could be inflated and knotted to provide a light, bouncy ball. A bladder alone did not last very long, so people began to protect the bladders in a shell made of animal skin cured to turn it into leather. This design worked so well that it is still used, but with modern, synthetic materials rather than animal products.

HEAVY GOING
Balls of the 1870s were often formed by stitching together eight segments of leather, the ends of which were secured by a central disk. They were heavy, and it was impossible to kick them any great distance. Heading the ball could even prove fatal, especially if it was raining and the ball absorbed water. For obvious reasons, heading was not a technique often used in those days. The dribbling game was the popular style, and the heavy ball was suitable for this kind of play.

Sections of leather sewn together

Manufacturers' names were first stencilled on balls in about 1900.

The lace for tightening the case is raised.

Interlocking panels of leather

Tool for lacing the ball tightly

Copper stencil

MADE TO MEASURE
This ball was used in March 1912, in the international match between Wales and England at Wrexham, Wales. England won the match 2–0. Made from a pig's bladder wrapped in cowhide, it is typical of the type of ball used for most of this century. The outside shell was laced up. The size and weight of soccer balls were standardized by 1912, but the balls still absorbed water and tended to lose their shape.

The colors are based on those of the French flag

Brand name marked on the ball with a stencil

WORLD CUP COLORS
The first World Cup balls to have a color other than black were used in the Finals in France in 1998. They had a shiny, synthetic coating to make them waterproof and incorporated a layer of foam between the latex bladder and the polyester skin. This let players pass and shoot quickly and also put spin and swerve on the ball. Like 75 percent of the world's soccer balls, they were made in the Sialkot region of Pakistan.

HEADING FOR TROUBLE
Balls like this were used in the 1966 World Cup Finals, at which time ball design had hardly changed in 50 years. The leather case was backed with a lining, a development of the 1940s that improved durability. The outside was painted with a pigment that helped repel some water from a rain-soaked field. Manufacturers had still not found a reliable alternative to lacing up the ball, so players risked injury when they headed the ball.

The handle is pushed into the cylinder to pump up the bladder.

The piston expels air from the pump.

The Nesthill brass pump

The Sykometer measures air pressure.

Pump is used when standing upright.

Pressure valve

Pump from 1893 equipment catalog

Tube to attach the pump to the ball's valve

PATCHING THINGS UP
This 1970s repair kit would have been used with a vinyl ball. The metal rod was heated and then inserted into the puncture to create a hole of the right size, into which a patch could be glued.

Pump is inserted straight into the ball.

Patch with "nipple" to fit the hole

Glue

Spare valve

Metal rod

BALL BOYS
This 17th century German engraving shows that inflated animal bladders have been used in ball games for a long time. The two men depicted are servants preparing a spare ball for their masters, who would have been playing pallone, a soccer game that was played in 17th century northern Europe.

1630 engraving made by Matthaus Merian the Older

FULL OF AIR
Over time, air escaped from a soccer ball's bladder, and a pump was used to reinflate it. Sometimes, the air pressure in a bladder was increased to improve the bounce of the ball. If a bladder was pumped up too high, it was likely to burst, so some pumps came with their own pressure gauge. These pumps date from about 1890.

Calcio balls are made of leather that is stitched together and then painted.

The use of two colors makes the Orkney ball flash in the air.

Alternative balls
Several different football games are played around the world. Each uses a ball particular to it. Some football games have existed for centuries. The balls may have features connected to a ceremonial aspect of the game, and involve decoration and color, or they may be designed to withstand harsh treatment. In some modern games the ball has evolved along with the game.

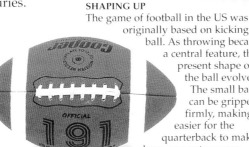

SHAPING UP
The game of football in the US was originally based on kicking a ball. As throwing became a central feature, the present shape of the ball evolved. The small ball can be gripped firmly, making it easier for the quarterback to make long, accurate passes.

BUILT TO LAST
In the Scottish Orkney Isles, a type of football game is played through the streets every New Year. The ball is much heavier than a normal soccer ball and is stuffed tightly with pieces of cork. This helps it last for several hours of play and allows it to float – a useful feature because a team can score a goal by throwing the ball into the sea.

MADE TO MATCH
Calcio, first played in Italy in the 16th century, was reintroduced to Florence in 1930. The game is played by teams of 27, all wearing medieval clothes and armor. Balls of various colors are used, including green, white, and red to match the costumes. Calcio balls are smaller than soccer balls, making it easier for the players to pick them up and throw them.

Soccer shoes

A 1950s painting of soccer shoes called *Christopher's Boots*, by Doris Brand

OF ALL SOCCER equipment, shoes have changed most over the past 100 years. Always the most expensive item of equipment, they remain an unaffordable luxury to many players around the world who have to play in bare feet. The fast, agile sport we see today would simply not be possible if soccer players had to use the heavy, cumbersome shoes worn up until the 1930s. Professionals then dreaded having to "break in" hard, new shoes, which involved a great deal of pain. They preferred to patch up an old pair again and again until they fell apart. In the first World Cup tournaments in the 1930s, the South American teams wore lighter, low-cut shoes, much to the astonishment of the Europeans. These began the trend toward the modern, high-tech boot.

MULTIPURPOSE SHOES
In the late 1800s, very few people playing soccer would have worn special footwear. These girl's shoes could also have been worn to school or in the house. The smooth soles, pronounced heel, and extremely high cut would have seriously constricted movement, but the ankle would have been well protected.

19th-century girls' shoes

1920s child's shoes

Playing soccer is a popular pastime with children.

MADE FOR THE JOB
By the 1920s, soccer shoes, like the "Manfield Hotspur," were being mass-produced for players of all ages. Children's shoes were designed just like adults', with reinforced toe caps and heels, some ankle protection, and leather cleats. Social conditions at the time, though, meant that most working-class families could not afford such equipment and, if they could, they would have handed down shoes from one child to another.

Extra foot support

Cotton laces

CLEATLESS SHOES
A 19th-century gentleman soccer player wore cleatless shoes, which would not have allowed for sharp turns or long passing. However, they were practical enough for the type of dribbling game favored by the great English amateur teams like the Corinthians. This style of play was dictated by the confined spaces used for soccer practice at many British private schools. Shoes like these would have doubled in weight when wet.

SHOES IN THE BATH
In 1910, these shoes were marketed as "Cup Final Specials," an early example of a soccer product being tied to a famous match. The wickerwork pattern on the toes was one of several designs that was thought to help a player control the ball – a major part of modern shoe design too. It was common for a player to wear a new pair of shoes in the bath for a few hours to soften the leather.

LOTS OF LACES
Paton's shoelaces, in various colors, were widely used from the 1930s onward. There was a constant demand for replacements because repeated soaking during matches, followed by drying out, caused the early cotton laces to perish and eventually snap.

PERSONALIZED SHOES
Shoes of a color other than black or brown are a feature of the modern game. Moustafa Hadji of Morocco was one of several players to wear a different color at the 1998 World Cup. However, this was not unknown in the past. Puma produced a white shoe in 1958, and England player Alan Ball was known for his white shoes a decade later.

Flexible ankle support

Laces were wrapped around the shoes for a closer fit.

White laces were common in the 1930s.

England's Tom Finney promoted these shoes

THE MODERN LOOK
The classic design of black with white trim, which is still used, began to be popular in the 1950s. The vertical strap on the instep remains from earlier designs. The shoes were becoming flexible enough to be worn without much breaking in. There was less protection around the ankle, which allowed players more freedom of movement but led to an increase in injuries. It was at this time that shoemakers began to use the name of famous players to sell their shoes.

THE DESIGNER AGE
A vast amount of money is spent on the research and development of modern shoes. Top-quality leather uppers, usually made from kangaroo hides, and light, synthetic soles combine to make shoes that last. They are comfortable and allow the best players to put amazing amounts of spin on the ball. Competition among manufacturers is intense, and huge amounts of money are spent on advertising.

Cleats are screwed into the sole.

Cleats and stuff

The number of cleats on the sole, and the way in which they are positioned, varies greatly. Longer cleats are needed if the field is wet and muddy; shorter ones are worn if the field is hard. The potential they have to cause injury has always been a concern to the game's governing bodies – in the 1930s, the wearing of illegal boots was an expulsion offense. Since 1900, one of the jobs of the referee or an assistant has been to check the cleats of every player entering the field of play. Anybody wearing shoes with sharp edges or protruding nails is not allowed to play.

Wooden hammer

Nails fixed to cleats

Separate nails

Key for tightening the cleats

THE FIRST CLEATS
Early soccer shoes were made entirely of leather. The cleats had to be hammered into the soles.

HARMFUL HAMMERS
Rubber cleats came next. They also needed nailing to the sole, and it was not long before the shoes were damaged.

ALL CHANGE!
Modern screw-in cleats are made of plastic or metal. Players can change their cleats at halftime, to adjust to changes in conditions.

Soccer uniforms

In the 19th century, both football and rugby players wore knee-length knickerbockers with no leg protection.

Sʜɪʀᴛꜱ, ꜱʜᴏʀᴛꜱ, and socks were described as the basis of a soccer uniform in the first rules of 1863, and they remain so today. The materials used for a soccer player's uniform have changed since then. Players in South America and Mediterranean countries needed clothing suitable for warm climates, so wool gave way to cotton and then artificial fibers. Cool fabrics that "breathe" are now the norm worldwide. Teams wear matching uniforms, or strips, on the field of play. The colors are the colors of the team, with which all the fans can identify. Most teams and International sides have a home and an away strip in case two teams wear the same colors.

DUTCH ORANGE
The Holland strip is unusual in being orange, and is recognized all around the world. The Dutch fans wear replica shirts and other orange clothes to form a mass of color at matches. Here, Marc Overmars is on the ball for Holland during the 1998 World Cup Finals.

WOOLLY SWEATERS
In the late 19th century, soccer jerseys were often made from wool. They tended to stretch out of shape and could become heavy in the rain because they soaked up water.

AWAY STRIP
In the 1966 World Cup final, the England team wore light cotton shirts with a round collar. Although England was playing at home, it did not wear its normal white home strip because West Germany was wearing white. England wore red instead.

LACE-UPS
At all levels of the game, teams began to wear matching strips. This black-and-white shirt was worn by a member of Newcastle United's team for the 1908 English FA Cup final. Newcastle still wear black and white. The shirt is made of thick cotton with a lace-up collar. Lace-up collars became fashionable again in the 1990s and were worn by Manchester United, among other teams.

AUSTRALIAN AMATEURS
This Australian shirt is made from wool with a cotton collar. It was worn in 1925 by the player Tommy Traynor. Shirts worn in International matches have symbolic importance. At the end of the game, the teams swap shirts with each other in a gesture of goodwill.

KEEPING COOL
Today, most shirts are designed to keep players cool and draw away excess moisture. This 1994 Brazil World Cup shirt is made of light, synthetic fabrics. With the energetic pace of modern games, such improvements are vital, especially for matches played in hot climates.

FAIR-WEATHER FRIENDS

By the early 20th century, manufacturers in many countries had begun to adapt the kit that British players had taken overseas with them in the 19th century. They produced lighter clothes more suited to warm climates. Short-sleeved shirts and deep V-neck collars became part of the typical Mediterranean look, as represented on this image from Valencia in Spain.

Early 1900s Spanish illustration

These socks are unusually decorative.

Women were not expected to head the ball.

Hoops and stripes are classic design features.

PULL YOUR SOCKS UP

These socks from the 1920s look just the same as modern ones, but they are made of wool. Modern socks are made of synthetic materials, making them more comfortable. Players keep up their socks with ties or elastic around the top. The ties can be made from strips of bandage or elasticated tape cut up into lengths. Towards the end of a grueling match, when players are prone to cramp, they may discard the tie-ups. Socks around the ankle can be a tell-tale sign of a tired player facing defeat.

High kicking was easier if shorts were above the knees

Cream flannel shorts from about 1900

Modern synthetic shorts with decorative side seams

Hard-wearing cotton shorts from the 1930s

Early 20th century French illustration

UNDER WRAPS

Until World War I, women soccer players had to keep their hair under a cap and hide their legs inside voluminous bloomers. In the 1910s, when many men were away at war, crowds flocked to see women's exhibition matches. This wider acceptance of ladies' soccer enabled women's teams to start wearing soccer uniforms that were similar to those worn by men and more suitable for the game.

SHORT STORY

Gentlemen amateurs in the 1860s played in full-length pants, but, as the game developed, players had to increase their speed and agility. Shorter pants cut just above the knee then became popular. The baggy style of soccer shorts of the 1930s was made famous by Alex James of Arsenal, England, "the wee man in the big shorts." This fashion was revived in the 1990s following a trend in the 1970s for tight shorts.

Accessories

INJURY AND DISCOMFORT were part of the game of soccer in its early days. When protective equipment and other accessories, such as hats, earmuffs, and belts, were introduced at the end of the 19th century, they helped distance the game from its rather violent past. Shinpads were developed in 1874 by a player called Samuel Widdowson, in response to the physical punishment that players suffered during games. Leg protectors are still worn, but other accessories are no longer used.

Buttoned tunic was an alternative to the more common shirt.

Leather buckles fasten these shinpads.

LASTING DESIGN
In the 1900s, players would have worn shinpads like these outside their socks, held in place with straps and buckles. The front section is made of leather and the back of cotton, with a stuffing of animal hair. This mix of materials was used in shinpads until the 1960s.

THE FIRST SHINPADS
The earliest shinpads were worn outside the socks and were extended to include ankle protectors, which rested on the top of the boot. Some, like these, had a suede covering, which was more prone to water damage than other types of leather. These heavy and inflexible pads date from the 1890s, about 20 years after shinpads became part of the soccer player's gear.

REINFORCED GUARDS
This figure is from a picture on the box of an early 20th century German soccer game. His shinpads, worn over the top of his socks and pants, appear to be strengthened with cane bars.

BELT UP
Decorative belts were a part of many youths' soccer gear until the 20th century. They spiffed up appearances by holding in the shirt and gave teams identity through the use of colors. Belts were also part of women's uniforms in the early 1900s.

Early 20th century schoolboys' belts

Woman's belt from 1895

ROOM TO MOVE
By 1910, ankle protection was no longer part of shinpad design, not because it was not needed, but because it restricted movement of the foot. Passing and running off the ball had become important parts of the game, requiring increased flexibility of the ankle. Players were therefore forced to sacrifice some protection. Cork was sometimes used to strengthen pads.

TIE-ON SHINPADS
Shinpads worn inside the socks had taken over by 1930. Laces, instead of buckles, were used for fastening, to prevent chafing on the players' legs. Many years later, tighter-fitting synthetic, rather than woolen, socks held the pads firmly in position, without the need for ties of any sort.

1980s shinpads were similar in shape to those from the 1930s.

Long laces to wrap around the leg twice

LIGHTWEIGHT PROTECTION
Modern shinpads look dramatically different from earlier models. They are shaped to fit the leg, using lightweight materials to give excellent protection. Even the delicate Achilles tendon at the back of the ankle is shielded. The revival of ankle protectors, after a gap of 100 years, brings shinpad design full circle.

KEEPING WARM
Gloves have become common, especially among players from hot countries, such as Brazil, who play in Europe, often in freezing temperatures. Players susceptible to hamstring and groin injuries are encouraged to wear Lycra shorts because they help to keep these important muscles warm.

Women wore hats to keep long hair out of the mud.

Stripes to match team colors

Brazilian star Emerson

Women's soccer hats

SOCCER PLAYER
This is a porcelain figure of a boy, made in the 1890s for export from Germany. Artistic depictions of soccer from this period often showed players wearing hats, even though they were becoming decorative rather than practical items.

Hand-painted German figure

HATS OFF!
These women's hats date from 1895, when women's soccer was still in its infancy. The fact that women played in hats does not mean that theirs was a gentler game. Like the men, many women players wore shinpads for protection.

Famous players

SOCCER IS A TEAM GAME. Teams and national sides inspire the greatest passion among fans, but a few players are so gifted and entertaining that they stand out from their teammates and draw thousands of extra people to games. Some great players are famous for their spirit of fair play, while others have been surrounded by controversy and bad publicity. But all the great players share an ability to change the course of a game through a moment of incredible individual skill.

GORDON BANKS (b. 1937)
English goalkeeper Gordon Banks is remembered for one save in particular – a spectacular effort that kept out Pele's header in the 1970 World Cup. Banks won 73 caps between 1963 and 1972 and would have won more, but for an eye injury.

JOHANN CRUYFF (b. 1947)
One of the few great players also to have become a successful manager, Cruyff was able to instill in his teams some of the style and tactical awareness that made him such a joy to watch. He played for Holland, Ajax, and Barcelona, Spain. He personified the concept of "total football" by floating all over the field and using his amazing balance and skill to open up defenses.

GERD MULLER (b. 1945)
Known as *"Der Bomber,"* Gerd Muller was an unlikely looking center-forward. He had an astonishing spring in his heels, which made up for his lack of height. He was a prolific goal scorer, with 68 goals in 62 games for West Germany. Most of his team soccer was played with Bayern Munich, Germany, for which he scored 365 goals.

Milla was a great entertainer, known for his flamboyant goal celebrations.

Roger Milla after scoring for Cameroon against Colombia in the 1990 World Cup

ROGER MILLA (b. 1952)
Twice African player of the year, Roger Milla of Cameroon was the first player to become famous worldwide playing for an African country. He was also the oldest player to appear and score in a World Cup final in 1994, aged 42.

BOBBY CHARLTON (b. 1937)
Manchester United star Bobby Charlton survived the Munich air crash that killed seven of his teammates in 1958. Known for the power and accuracy of his shooting, he was invaluable in England's 1966 World Cup win. He was knighted in 1994.

Eusebio practices ball control in training.

DIEGO MARADONA (b. 1960)

Maradona was the best player of his generation and one of the most controversial. He had a tremendous ability to inspire his teammates, most notably when leading Argentina to the 1986 World Cup and Napoli to two Serie A titles in Italy in the late 1980s. His magical left foot and strength in possession were his main assets.

Maradona's low center of gravity gave him excellent balance.

In the 1986 World Cup against England, Maradona scored two goals – one a handball that should have been nullified, the other a dazzling solo effort.

Eusebio scored 38 goals in 46 international games.

EUSEBIO (b. 1942)

Although he was born in Mozambique, Eusebio was snapped up by Benfica of Lisbon, Portugal, and went on to play for Portugal, as did several other talented players. He starred in the 1962 European Cup final, scoring twice as Benfica beat Real Madrid, Spain, 5–3. Eusebio was respected all over the world for his fair play and dignity as well as for his soccer talent.

GARRINCHA (b. 1933)

Nicknamed "the Little Bird," Garrincha had polio as a child. He overcame his disability to become one of the quickest and most elusive wingers the game has seen. He played on the right-hand side of Brazil's legendary 1958 forward line. In 1962, he made up for the absence of the injured Pele with some brilliant performances, helping Brazil retain the World Cup.

Meazza (*below right*) shakes hands with Hungarian captain, Sarosi, before the 1938 World Cup final.

Like many of the greatest players, Maradona liked to be number 10.

GUISEPPE MEAZZA (b. 1910)

Italian Giuseppe Meazza won two World Cup winner's medals, in 1934 and 1938. He was respected as a creator and scorer of goals from his inside-forward position. In 1938, he organized the Italian team when the coach, Pozzo, was ordered to leave the bench and sit in the stands. He spent his best years at Internazionale of Milan, Italy, and won 53 caps.

Maradona's magical footwork entertained and amazed the fans.

Continued on next page

MARCO VAN BASTEN (b. 1964)
Van Basten of Holland scored one of the greatest goals of all time at the European Championship final in 1988 – a volley from wide of the goal. Sadly, an ankle injury cut short his career.

LUIS SUAREZ (B. 1935)
Considered one of the best Spanish soccer players, Luis Suarez dominated the midfield for Barcelona, Spain, in the late 1950s. By the mid-1960s, he was playing a key part in Italian Inter Milan's new *catenaccio* system – a lineup heavy on defense with only two forward players. He was famous for his fast breaks out of defense and accurate passes. Suarez went on to be manager of Spain at the 1990 World Cup.

Kopa was the greatest French player of the 1950s.

Kopa was known for his careful ball control and well-thought-out passing.

Van Basten was the best center-forward of the late 1980s.

RAYMOND KOPA (b. 1931)
Creative midfielder Raymond Kopa made his name with the French team, Reims. He led them to the first European Cup final in 1956, where they lost to Spain's Real Madrid. Kopa played for France at the 1958 World Cup and was named European Footballer of the Year in 1959.

The two defenders are playing for the Italian team Roma.

Roma defenders are left in Platini's wake.

STANLEY MATTHEWS (b. 1915)
England's Stanley Matthews was known for his dribbling skills. One of his finest performances was in Blackpool's 4–3 win over Bolton in the 1953 English FA Cup final. He won 84 caps and was still playing soccer for Stoke City at the age of 50. He was knighted in 1965.

LEV YASHIN (b. 1929)
Always outfitted in black, Lev Yashin was rivaled only by Gordon Banks as the greatest goalkeeper of his era. He played for the Soviet Union in three World Cups and is, to this day, the only goalkeeper to have been named European Footballer of the Year.

Between them, Puskas and Di Stefano scored seven goals in the European Cup final in 1960.

FRANZ BECKENBAUER (b. 1945)

Beckenbauer's intelligence shone on the field as he dictated play from a deep sweeper position. Together with Johann Cruyff, he is one of the few soccer-playing legends to achieve similar success as a manager. Having captained West Germany at the 1974 World Cup, he managed the team when it won again in 1990.

FERENC PUSKAS (b. 1927)

The star of Hungary's famous team of the 1950s, Ferenc Puskas was part of the Hungarian team that beat England 6–3 at Wembley in 1953. He joined Real Madrid of Spain in 1958. Puskas strongly favored his left foot, scoring a wealth of stunning goals for both club and country.

ALFREDO DI STEFANO (b. 1926)

When Real Madrid dominated European soccer in the 1950s, Di Stefano was one of its star players. His stamina enabled him to contribute all over the field. He and Puskas formed one of soccer's legendary double acts.

MICHEL PLATINI (b. 1955)

Platini was one of those players who seemed happy to take the weight of a nation's expectations on his shoulders. He captained France in the 1984 European Championships, and the team won the tournament for the first time. Platini was an attacking midfielder who often finished as top scorer at Italian club Juventus.

Michel Platini playing for Juventus

Platini had the speed and foresight to move forward into space

PELE (b. 1940)

Many people's choice of the greatest player of all would be Pele. He was king of Brazilian soccer from the late 1950s to early 1970s. He overcame constant fouling by frustrated defenders to score more than 1,000 goals for the Brazilian club Santos, American soccer team New York Cosmos, and the Brazilian national team. Despite being plagued by injury, his obvious love of playing and enthusiasm make him a perfect role model for the game of soccer.

Medals and caps

IT IS THE AIM OF ALL soccer players to play well and win each game. Those lucky enough to win a championship are awarded a medal as a mark of their achievement. Those good enough to be picked to play for their country win a cap. Medals and caps have been part of the game since the 19th century and are still valued rewards today. At the highest level, success can be measured by the number of caps a player has, and passing the "100 cap" mark is considered exceptional service to the national team. Thomas Ravelli of Sweden won 138 caps – a record for a European.

Argentine pot made from a dried eggplant trimmed with silver

Ornate silver dagger

Norwegian silver spoon

Argentine silver implement

Medals

As with military medals for soldiers, soccer players are rewarded with medals for helping their side, not for a moment of personal glory. Medals are awarded at all levels of soccer, professional and amateur. They are mementoes by which players can remember their glory days, and can become valuable collectors' items.

GOOD SPORT
Before organized leagues were established, soccer medals were often awarded for sportsmanship as well as victories. The full-back C. Duckworth was given this medal for "gentlemanly and successful play" in the 1883–84 season.

WITH COMPLIMENTS
This "complimentary medal for defeating all comers" in the 1884–85 season was awarded to B. Robinson of Accrington Stanley.

PRECIOUS GIFTS
As well as caps and medals, International players are sometimes presented with gifts by opposing soccer associations. The England team players received silver spoons when they faced Norway in 1949. The Argentine FA gave the England team members ceremonial daggers and other silver items on their first visit to Wembley, England, in 1951.

English v. Scottish League 1893

FA Cup runners-up 1893

DOUBLE
This group of medals belonged to R. H. Howarth of the Preston North End "Invincibles." The team won the League and the FA Cup in 1888–89, achieving the first English "double."

Lancashire Cup winners 1887

TROPHY TRIUMPH
This plaque was made to commemorate an International match between France and England in 1947. All the English players received a plaque after winning the match 3–0.

CLUB STRIKERS
Some clubs strike their own medals to mark a special achievement of their players. Preston North End awarded this one to their players for winning the English Second Division.

1909 Hungarian medal

CHAMPIONS
This medal was awarded to a player for success in the 1914-15 season.

AMATEUR
This 1920s medal was given to a successful amateur player.

ARSENAL STAR
This 1930s medal may have belonged to soccer star Alex James.

PLAY-OFF PRIZES
Medals have been presented to the winners of the third- and fourth-place play-off match at every World Cup Finals, except 1930 and 1950. At France '98, Croatia won third-place medals, defeating Holland 2–1 with goals from Robert Prosinecki and Davor Suker.

HUNGARY FOR SUCCESS
Hungary was one of the first European countries to take to soccer. The Hungarians copied the way other countries ran the game, including the awarding of medals. This medal was awarded to the members of an International team after a match against Austria in 1909.

Caps

A colored cap was once the only way of showing to which side a player belonged. Then, in 1872, the FA ruled that teams should wear distinctive shirts. In 1886, it was suggested that caps be awarded to players each time they played for their country. Today, they are given to every member of a national team, including substitutes. Often, only one cap is awarded for a series of games, so a player with 50 "caps" has fewer actual ones.

Tassels are added for decoration.

HOME CAP
This Welsh cap was awarded for the 1903–04 Home International matches among England, Scotland, Northern Ireland, and Wales. This tournament took place every year until 1984.

CAREY'S CAP
The great defender Johnny Carey won this cap when he played for Ireland against Poland and Switzerland in 1938. Carey won 36 caps.

Welsh national crest – a dragon

1903-4

Details of different matches can be embroidered into each panel.

Soccer caps are usually made of velvet.

SCHOOL COLORS
Soccer caps were first awarded in English private schools. "Colors," in the form of caps, were given to the most able players in each year.

IN TRAINING
It is not only players who are rewarded for their efforts. Trainer Will Scott received this medal when the English and Scottish Leagues met at Celtic Park, Glasgow, Scotland, in November 1931.

The date covers games from a whole season.

Northern Ireland had its own team from 1921.

WORLD CUP
The biggest soccer achievement is victory in the World Cup final. This is a replica of the Jules Rimet medal given to West Germany's winning players in 1954.

WAR GAMES
Throughout World War II, famous International players took part in exhibition matches arranged to boost public morale. In 1946, Tom Finney was given this set of three medals after appearing in a match in Antwerp, Belgium.

PROMOTIONAL MEDAL
By the 1950s, businesses had started to commemorate a range of soccer events. The French newspaper *Le Soir* made this medal to mark a club tour of Austria in 1953.

AFRICAN CUP
This medal was presented to the winners of the first African Nations' Cup in 1957. The competition was held in Khartoum, Sudan, and only Sudan, Ethiopia, and Egypt took part. Egypt beat Ethiopia 4–0 in the final.

39

Famous teams

ITALIAN ZEBRAS
Juventus is the most successful Italian team and enjoys great support outside Turin. Nicknamed the Zebras for its black-and-white striped shirt, Juventus won the European Cup in 1985 and 1996.

Sᴏᴍᴇ ᴛᴇᴀᴍꜱ ɪɴꜱᴘɪʀᴇ the greatest loyalty and passion from soccer fans, more so even than national teams. In every country, certain big teams attract followers from beyond their local areas and tend to dominate their domestic leagues and cups. Success for these teams often continues because financial backing ensures a steady supply of good new players. In all corners of the world, people swear allegiance to Barcelona or Liverpool, Flamengo or Milan, although they may never be able to attend a game involving their team.

BRAVO BENFICA
Only Porto and Sporting Lisbon rival Benfica in the Portuguese League. Benfica also has had some notable victories on the more competitive European stage. Benfica was the great team of the early 1960s, winning two European Cups, in 1961 and 1962, and reaching but losing three further finals.

This bronze depicts Benfica's symbol, an eagle.

Figure of the ancient Greek hero Ajax forms the basis of the team's crest.

MIGHTY MARSEILLE
In 1993, Marseille, France, led by the attacking threat of Allen Boksic and Rudi Voller, beat AC Milan of Italy 1–0 to lift the European Cup. French administrators, such as long-time FIFA president Jules Rimet, have always had a large role in soccer, but it was 1993 before a French team won a European trophy.

LONDON LADIES
Netty Honeyball was the force behind the first great women's team in the 1890s. The British Ladies Club drew large crowds for its exhibition games in London at a time when the capital was lagging behind the North and Midlands of England with regard to soccer.

YOUNG TALENT
In the 1970s, Dutch team Ajax's policy to develop its own young players bore fruit. The players, including the star Johann Cruyff, helped Ajax to three consecutive European Cup wins in the 1970s, and some of them helped the national team in two World Cups. Despite regularly selling its best players, the team returned to the forefront of European soccer in the mid-1990s.

The team Ajax was formed in Amsterdam in 1900.

POWELL

BUSBY BABES
English team Manchester United started life as Newton Heath. It changed its name in 1902. The Munich air disaster of 1958, in which eight of manager Matt Busby's young players died, inspired sympathy around the world. Since then, the team has won two European Cups – in 1968 and 1999.

Baines card from the 1890s shows fullback, Jack Powell.

THE GOLDEN YEARS
Bayern Munich followed Ajax as the leading European team in the early 1970s. It won three consecutive European Cups with the help of players such as Franz Beckenbauer, Gerd Muller, and Sepp Maier, who were also important to the German national team.

Paul Breitner of Bayern Munich in 1974

Dominguez, the goalkeeper – from Argentina.

Alfredo Di Stefano, the leader of the team.

Francisco Gento, the fast left winger.

REAL RIVALRY
In the late 1950s, Real Madrid, Spain, possibly had the greatest club ever. Legends such as Di Stefano and Puskas inspired this Spanish team to win the first five European Cups. Real Madrid has a spectacular stadium – the Bernabeu – and a bitter rivalry with Barcelona.

THE RED DEVILS
This picture shows the players Cagna and Rios of Independiente, Argentina, in 1995. In 1964, Independiente was the first Argentine team to win the South American team competition, the Copa Libertadores. The Red Devils went on to win the competition four more times between 1972 and 1975.

The fans

GONE BANANAS
In England in the late 1980s, there was a craze for taking large inflatable objects to matches. Fans waved bananas, fish, and fried eggs in the crowd to show their support for their teams.

For all the talent displayed by the players on the field, it is the fans who have made soccer the biggest game in the world. From the last years of the 19th century, working people began to have enough free time to attend sports events. They created an atmosphere of excitement and expectation, and large crowds became an important part of a match. Today, soccer is the most widely watched sport in the world. Fans are more eager than ever to show their support for team and country in a range of noisy and colorful ways.

Manchester City, England, pennant

Preston North End, England, rosette

Holland scarf

Lazio, Italy, scarf

CLUB COLOURS
Colours are a vital part of the bond between a team and its supporters. Once, people made rosettes for big matches and displayed pennants. Now, fans often wear a scarf to show their loyalty.

PERFECT VIEW
In their desperation to see a game, fans are not always put off by the "sold out" signs. In the 19th century, before large-scale stands were built, trees provided a convenient spot from which to watch a popular match.

RARE COLLECTION
Fans have always collected objects bearing images of soccer. Today the items probably feature their favorite team but, in the past, designs were based on more general soccer scenes. Collecting autographs is also a popular hobby and offers a rare opportunity to meet star players.

Jack Rowley, forward

John Aston, full-back

Johnny Carey, full-back

Matt Busby, manager

Child's money box

1950s autograph book containing signatures of famous figures of Manchester United, England.

Wooden pencil case

During the war, the sound of the bell warned people of an air raid.

Air-raid patrolman's rattle

Air-raid patrolman's bell

Adult's rattle

Rattles were originally used as bird scarers.

Top section moves around and around horizontally.

"Rattling" noise created at the handle

Child's rattle

NOISY SUPPORT

Rattles were part of the atmosphere at games until the 1960s. When the horizontal section of the rattle is whirled around the "clicker" on the handle, it produces a loud rattling noise. Since the 1960s, organized chanting has become more common. Modern safety regulations restrict what items may be taken into the stadium, and rattles are no longer allowed.

Child's rattle painted with a soccer scene

WAR CRY

Fans have taken bells and rattles to matches to express their support since before 1940. This bell and rattle were part of an air-raid patrolman's equipment in England World War II. In 1946, after the war, a Derby County fan took them to matches during Derby's run to the English FA Cup final.

WORLD BEATERS

Brazilian fans were famous for their noisy support long before the rest of the world discovered paints and drums. They produce a samba beat on their drums and blow their whistles. As the noise echoes around the stands, the fans dance to accompany the action, especially if their team is winning.

AFRICAN PAINTING

Face painting has become commonplace at major international matches, adding to the color and spectacle of the occasion. Here, two Zambian fans, painted to reflect the team's colours, enjoy an African Nations Cup match. Face painting is particularly popular with Dutch, Danish, and Japanese fans.

Game day

This is a scoreboard from an early 20th century· French soccer game.

THE ATMOSPHERE of a big game, the sound of the crowd, and the closeness of the players combine to make going to a live soccer game quite addictive. Even though soccer is now widely shown on television, millions of fans still go to the game. Many supporters, like players, are extremely superstitious and follow the same routine every time they attend a game. The fans and the noisy support they give their team are essential to the game of soccer. It is vital that teams continue to improve comfort and safety for their fans, so that they keep on coming back.

ALL DRESSED UP
This photo shows fans of West Ham, England, preparing to travel to the 1923 FA Cup final, the first to be held at Wembley. Many more than the official attendance of 123,000 crammed into the stadium. Notice the neat and formal appearance of the supporters.

In the 1988 European Championship final, Holland beat the Soviet Union 2-0.

Holograms and complicated designs are now used to deter ticket forgeries.

TICKETS PLEASE
Tickets are essential in controlling access to games. Years ago, this was necessary only at cup finals and World Cup matches. Tickets were issued for general areas in the stadium. Now that terraces, areas for standing spectators, are being phased out in favor of seating, each match ticket corresponds to a particular seat.

READING MATTER
The earliest programs were simple one-sheet items, giving only team lineups. As soccer became more popular, further elements were added, such as a message from the manager and background information on the opposition. Glossy, full-color brochures, largely paid for by advertising, are produced for tournaments such as the European Championships.

LET ME ENTERTAIN YOU
To make going to a game even more enjoyable, particularly for a family audience, teams and governing bodies provide extra entertainment before kick-off and at halftime. In the past, this may have taken the form of a brass band, but modern crowds expect something more elaborate. The opening ceremony at France '98 featured giant inflatable soccer balls.

A FAMILY AFFAIR
In the US, a trip to a sporting event is usually a family day out, and the stadiums have good facilities for everybody. There is a lot of razzmatazz at the Major League Soccer games. Cheerleaders and music keep the crowds well entertained. This is game day at the Kansas City Wizards' stadium.

1903 FA official's patch

Official patch from 1905

The patches are made of cloth and decorated with gold brocade.

FA patch from 1898

The English three lions motif

BACKSTAGE PASS
Away from the mass of spectators, there are certain areas of the stadium, such as the boardroom, where access is strictly controlled. These patches, from 1898–1905, would have been sewn on blazers and worn by Football Association officials. These days, executive boxes have become a feature of many stadiums.

Patch worn at 1899 England v. Scotland International

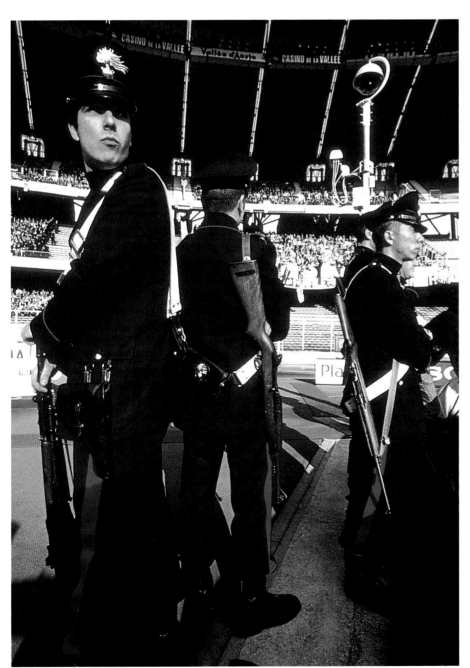

CROWD CONTROL
Police attend soccer matches to ensure the safety of everybody at the game. Police, like these Italian officers at a Juventus game, may need to take a hard line with unruly fans, and sometimes use horses or dogs to help them control large crowds. They may also control traffic and escort supporters to and from the game.

COMING HOME
This drawing comes from a postcard from the early 20th century. The caption on the card says, "Our team's lost by – goals to – ." Space is left on the card for fans to fill in the score. Somehow, the depression of defeat is always replaced by excitement and high hopes when the next game comes around.

The stadium

TWIN TOWERS
The famous Twin Towers at Wembley Stadium in England will not be part of the new stadium being built for the 21st century.

As CROWDS GREW EVER larger in the late 19th century, soccer teams realized that they would have to build permanent venues in which to hold their games. Stadiums became a necessity. They provided fans with shelter and a decent view of the game. They also created an atmosphere that added greatly to the game-day experience. A series of stadium disasters over the years, in places such as Scotland, Peru, and Russia, finally led to widespread belief that standing areas should be replaced by stands with seats, for the safety of spectators.

SHEFFIELD WEDNESDAY F.C.

THEN THERE WAS LIGHT...
Floodlights were first used in 1878, but they didn't become standard at professional games until the 1950s. The most common form of stadium lighting was on tall pylons in the corners of the stadium. Today, lights are often placed in rows along the stand roof.

CROWD SAFETY
On April 15, 1989, the FA Cup semifinal at Hillsborough, Sheffield, was the scene of the worst disaster in English soccer history. More than 90 Liverpool fans died in a devastating crowd crush. The resulting report began a major leap forward in stadium safety – to prevent a similar disaster from ever happening again.

WORLD CUP WONDER
The Maracana Stadium in Rio de Janeiro, Brazil, is named after a river that runs nearby. It was built for the 1950 World Cup. It is a huge concrete oval and has remained a source of wonder despite problems with its decaying structure. All the teams in Rio de Janeiro have their own grounds, but use the Maracana for big games. With its 120,000 capacity, it is one of the biggest stadiums in the world.

Lights along the top of the roof

STANDING TALLER
Barcelona, Spain, moved from Les Corts Stadium to the spectacular Nou Camp in 1957. Improvements for the 1982 World Cup and 1992 Olympics have increased the staggering height of the stands. The Nou Camp was paid for by the team's members.

PATH TO THE FIELD
The tunnel is more than just a route to the field. It is the place where players psych themselves up for the game and give in to their superstitions. Many insist on taking the same place in the line every time. Others put on their shirts only at the last moment.

The roof "hangs" from this crossbar.

The pylon is integral to the structure of the stand.

KEEPING UP TO DATE
Modern stands are designed using computer models to ensure that everybody has a good view. The space between seats is a difficult issue. More space means greater comfort, but it reduces the capacity of the stand. Designs, such as faces, are often picked out in the seats.

FANS ON THEIR FEET
Before all-seat stadiums were introduced, fans stood packed together on terraces. Far more fans could get in to watch a game and it is how the majority of people have watched games for much of soccer's history. Children were often passed over the heads of the crowd to the front to give them a better view.

STATE OF THE ART
The Stade de France is in St. Denis, north of Paris. It was built for the 1998 World Cup, and 80,000 spectators watched the opening game there between Brazil and Scotland. The stadium was widely praised for its dramatic design. The roof, enclosing the field in a continuous curve, creates an amphitheater effect, which has always been popular in European and South American stadiums.

Several tiers of seats

Field level openings for emergency vehicles

Revolving billboards around the field

The World Cup

THE SOCCER WORLD CUP is one of the greatest sports events of our time. The first World Cup was held in Uruguay in 1930, 26 years after FIFA first discussed the idea. In the early days, some teams were unable to travel to the host country, but by the 1950s, long-distance travel was becoming much easier and quicker. As the tournament became more accessible, it grew in popularity. The 1950 World Cup final at Maracana Stadium in Rio de Janeiro was attended by 200,000 people. In 1958, Brazilian teenager Pele became the first global soccer superstar. Since then, interest in the World Cup has boomed.

MANY MASCOTS
Every World Cup since 1966 has had a mascot. They appear as life-size figures at matches and scaled-down promotional or commercial images. This is Pique, from Mexico '86.

WORLD FIRST
Uruguay offered to pay travel and accommodation expenses to the 13 visiting teams at the first World Cup. Only four European teams made the long journey, joining the seven South American teams.

1954 – Switzerland. West Germany beat Hungary 3–2 in one of the great upsets in World Cup history.

1958 – Sweden. Brazil beat Sweden 5–2. Brazil is the only team to have played in every Finals tournament.

1950 – Brazil. Uruguay beat Brazil 2–1, in the first tournament after World War II.

1962 – Chile. Brazil beat Czechoslovakia 3–1, with Garrincha taking center stage after Pele was injured.

1938 – France. Italy beat Hungary 4–2, inspired by its star inside-forward, Meazza.

1966 – England. West Germany lost 2–4 to England in extra time, with Geoff Hurst scoring the first hat trick in a final.

1934 – Italy. Czechoslovakia lost 1–2 to Italy. Uruguay did not defend its crown, the only time this has happened.

1970 – Mexico. Brazil beat Italy 4–1 and were one of the greatest teams of all time.

1930 – Uruguay. Beating Argentina 4–2, Uruguay was the first of many host countries to win the Cup.

1974 – West Germany. Holland was beaten 2–1 by West Germany, which came back from being a goal behind.

VARIOUS VENUES
Competition to hold the World Cup Finals is always fierce because it brings visitors and publicity to the host country. The Finals in 2002, in Japan and South Korea, will be the first shared tournament and the first to be held outside Europe and the Americas.

Argentina '78 is remembered for the tickertape in the River Plate Stadium.

Mexico was the first country to host two Finals.

The Italia '90 mascot was called Ciao.

1978 – Argentina. Holland lost 1–3 to Argentina, leaving the Dutch as the best team never to have won the World Cup.

1982 – Spain. Italy beat West Germany 3–1, its striker Paolo Rossi finishing as leading scorer.

1986 – Mexico. Argentina beat West Germany 3–2, in a tournament dominated by Diego Maradona.

1990 – Italy. West Germany beat Argentina 1–0 in a defensive, bad-tempered final.

1998 – France. Brazil was beaten 3–0 by France in an amazingly one-sided match.

1994 – US. Brazil beat Italy 3–2 on penalties after a 0–0 draw and became the only team to have won four World Cups.

The figure is a winged seraphim.

WANDERING TROPHY

The first World Cup trophy was designed by a French sculptor, Abel Lafleur. It was later named in honor of the president of FIFA, Jules Rimet. The trophy was stolen before the 1966 tournament in England and was found in a park by a dog named Pickles. Brazil was presented with the trophy to keep in 1970, but it was stolen again and has not been seen since.

The trophy is made of solid gold.

The engraving on the trophy is in French.

Jules Rimet trophy

In 1994, American fans turned out in force to watch the matches.

The fans at Italia '90 provided more drama than some of the matches.

Copa del Mundo de la FIFA

Programma

JULES RIMET CUP
WORLD CHAMPIONSHIP
ENGLAND 1966 JULY 11-30

ESPAÑA 82
EDICIÓN EXCLUSIVA PARA ESPAÑA

Sweden, the host team, made it to the final in 1958 but was overpowered by the Brazilian super team

Guide
The World Championship in Football 1958
Sweden 8-29 · 6

STOCKHOLM
GOTEBORG
HALSINGBORG
MALMO

Coupe Jules Rimet

READ ALL ABOUT IT

Programs for the World Cup are different from the team variety, in that they usually cover the whole tournament rather than a specific match. They contain information about the competing teams and are printed in several languages. These programs are from Sweden '58, England '66, Spain '82, Italy '90, and US '94.

Didi

Pele was 17 in 1958.

Garrincha

THE BEAUTIFUL GAME

The 1958 final saw Brazil emerge as one of the World Cup's greatest teams. Its forward lineup was among the strongest in the game's history. Garrincha, Didi, Vava, Pele, and Zagalo drove the team to victory. Mario Zagalo later became the national team manager and was in charge when Brazil won again in 1970 and 1994.

Vava played at center-forward.

Zagalo, the left-winger scored the fourth goal in the final.

49

Continued on next page

WE MUST HAVE THE WORLD CUP

This was the poster for the 1962 Finals in Chile. A series of earthquakes marred the days before the tournament, but the hosts were determined. President of the Chilean FA, Carlos Dittborn, said, "We have nothing. That is why we must have the World Cup." Chile overcame the doubts of some European teams by staging a successful event. There was more trouble on the field than off it, particularly in the "Battle of Santiago" between Italy and Chile. Italy finished the game with nine men.

CAMPEONATO MUNDIAL DE FUTBOL
WORLD FOOTBALL CHAMPIONSHIP
CHAMPIONNAT MONDIAL DE FOOTBALL
COUPE JULES RIMET
CHILE 1962

World Cup Willie inspired a World Cup theme song by Lonnie Donnegan.

Globe forms the top of the trophy

The Union Jack flag represents Great Britain, not just England.

Designed by Italian Silvio Gazzaniga, the trophy is made of solid 18-carat gold.

The real trophy is 20 in (50.8 cm) high and weighs 20 lbs (9 kg.)

World Cup Willie was a lion, inspired by the three lions on the England uniform.

Replica of the World Cup trophy

MASCOTS FOR MONEY

World Cup Willie was the first World Cup mascot. Designed for the 1966 tournament in England, he represented the increase in commercialism. Since then tournament mascots, such as Ciao of Italy '90 and Footix of France '98, have appeared on official posters and been sold in many forms.

NEW LOOK CUP

The present World Cup trophy was made for the 1974 Finals in West Germany. Having won for the third time in 1970, Brazil had been allowed to keep the Jules Rimet trophy for good. The new trophy was commissioned by FIFA, despite an offer from Brazil to provide a trophy named after FIFA president, Sir Stanley Rous.

Argentina '78

THINKING POSITIVE
In 1978, host Argentina inspired its passionate fans with its positive attitude. The star of its winning team was Mario Kempes, who played team soccer in Europe.

ENTHUSIASTIC AMERICA
Despite having no strong tradition of professional soccer, the US hosted a successful World Cup Finals in 1994. Large and enthusiastic crowds attended all the games. This is a ticket for the game between Italy and Mexico, played at the former RFK Stadium, now the Jack Kent Cooke Stadium, home of American football team the Washington Redskins.

Information pack for Spain 1982

Spanish Football Federation crest

A pack of cards illustrating the stadiums

HARD WORK FOR HOSTS
A country bids to hold the World Cup several years in advance. It tries to convince FIFA that it will be able to stage a successful tournament. It has to produce information about all aspects of the tournament, including the stadiums, transportation networks, accommodations, and media facilities.

Fabien Barthez, France

The balls are brightly colored for the benefit of TV audiences.

Each ball contains a slip of paper with a team written on it.

Ronaldo, Brazil

Lilian Thuram, France

WHO PLAYS WHOM?
Plastic balls like these are used to make the draw for the World Cup Finals. It is a fair way to decide who plays whom. The number of competing teams has steadily increased from 13 in 1930 to 32 in 1998. The present system ensures that every team gets to play three games in the first round. Then, for the rest of the tournament, games are played on an elimination basis, until only two remain for the grand final.

IN THE BAG
This bag is a promotional item for the 2002 World Cup, to be staged jointly by Japan and South Korea. This will be the first shared tournament and the first to be held in Asia. Demand is sure to increase for smaller countries to benefit from this arrangement.

FRANCE IN ACTION
Brazil was expected to retain its title in 1998, but doubts surrounding Ronaldo's fitness to play seemed to distract the team in the final. The goalkeeper Fabien Barthez was one of many members in the victorious French team who enhanced his reputation with a brilliant performance throughout the tournament.

Cups and trophies

OLYMPIC SOCCER
This patch is from the 1956 Olympic Games. The Olympics featured demonstration soccer games from 1896. The first official Olympic tournament was in 1908.

THE MOMENT WHEN a team captain is presented with a trophy and holds it up to the fans is the crowning glory of any campaign. Cups and trophies are the marks of success, and the managers of many modern teams know that, if they are to hold on to their job, their team has to win a competition. For clubs like Real Madrid in Spain, Benfica in Portugal, and Bayern Munich in Germany, finishing as runners-up is considered a failure. The desire to make money has led to the creation, in recent years, of many new competitions, some of which do not have the same prestige as older tournaments such as the European Cup and the Copa America.

TEAM TALK
The European Cup was originally for the champions of each country's league. Now some lower placed teams compete. The competition was first held in 1956. At the 1985 final at the Heysel Stadium in Brussels, Belgium, 39 people died. A safety wall collapsed as fans of Juventus, Italy, and Liverpool, England, fought each other.

Program for the 1985 European Cup final

Corner flags used as decoration

EARLY CUP
This decorative, silver-plated trophy from the 1870s is an example of an early soccer cup. After the FA Cup was started in 1872, local tournaments for small teams began to be set up all over England and Scotland along the same lines.

FULL HOUSE
In the 1999 Women's World Cup in the US, teams played in front of capacity crowds. The final was held in the Rose Bowl in Passadena, California. Here, US player Cindy Parlow rides a tackle in the final against China. The US won, to secure its second World Cup victory.

The gold-plated Women's World Cup trophy has a soccer ball at the top.

Holding the trophy aloft is a proud moment.

WOMENS' WORLD CUP
The first Women's World Cup took place in China in 1991. The final was held in Guangzhou, where the US beat Norway 2–1. The tournament went from strength to strength, and the next two events, in 1995 and 1999, drew large crowds. This is the trophy awarded to the US in 1999.

LITTLE TIN IDOLS
The first FA Cup, on the left, was known as the Little Tin Idol. It was stolen from a store display in 1895 and was never recovered. The present FA Cup, on the right, was made in Bradford, England, in 1912.

The silver UEFA trophy is decorated with a design of men playing soccer.

Names of previous winners engraved around the base

FROM STRENGTH TO STRENGTH
The African Nations Cup has been held every two years since 1957. It has grown from humble beginnings, and as many as 16 teams now take part. Egyptian striker Hassan Hossam is pictured here after his team's 1998 triumph over the defending champions, South Africa. This was Egypt's fourth African Nations title.

COPA AMERICA CUP
First held in 1910, the Copa America is the oldest major international competition. It was originally played only by South American countries, but in recent years, Mexico and the US have also taken part. Uruguay won the first official Copa America in 1917 and, along with Argentina, has been the most successful team over the years. Brazil has not always played its strongest team. Since 1987, the tournament has been held every two years.

SECOND BEST
The UEFA (Union of European Football Associations) Cup was originally known as the Inter City Fairs Cup. The first competition was played over three years, beginning in 1955. Barcelona beat London 8–2 in the two-legged final. When the European Cup Winner's Cup was abolished in 1999, only two European team competitions remained. The strongest sides qualify for the European Cup, and the next best play in the UEFA Cup.

The Copa America was conceived by Chile, Uruguay, Brazil, and Argentina

Playing the game

GENERATIONS OF children have had their first contact with soccer through toys such as Fussball, card games, and Subbuteo. The popularity of soccer means that, as with other merchandise, there is money to be made from developing new products with a soccer theme. This drives manufacturers and inventors to come up with a vast range of games based on soccer, far more than on any other sport. The simplicity of the toys from the past, shown here, contrasts sharply with the speed and excitement of modern computer games. Today, children and adults can experience virtual soccer games and act out the roles of their favorite players and teams on Playstations and in computer games.

Two lead "kicking" figures from the early 20th century

This game was advanced for its time.

Points are lost if a marble is trapped here.

Marbles are fired up this chute.

BALL ROLLING
This handheld toy was made in the early 20th century. It involves rolling the ball bearing into one of the small holes.

IN THE TRENCHES
Trench Soccer was produced for British soldiers fighting in World War I. The player must move a ball bearing safely past the German generals to score.

SOCCER MATCHBOX
This is the world's **smallest** soccer game, probably made in Japan in the 1930s for small children. When the matchbox is opened, a spring is released and the players leap up.

PINBALL
In this bagatelle game from the 1950s, players shoot marbles around the board using a spring in the bottom-right-hand corner. Points are scored or lost according to where the marbles stop.

Ball for the Kick game

Downward pressure on one leg causes the other leg to kick.

The cards feature different positions and parts of the game.

KICK FIGURES
These figures come from a tabletop game called Kick, made in about 1900. A green cloth field, and goals with nets are included. Players make the mechanical soccer players kick by pressing them down on the table. They are moved around by hand – a feature also used in more modern soccer toys.

Combination of red and white is a classic football strip

Key fits into the ball to wind it up

SNAP!
This rare pack of snap cards from the early 20th century features soccer characters. In snap, players aim to collect all the cards. They turn over cards until two identical ones turn up together. The first player to shout "Snap!" takes the pile.

CLOCKWORK PLAYER
This tin-plate clockwork toy was made in Germany in the early 1950s. When wound up with a key, the figure moves forward, as if dribbling the ball. The shirt, with its loosely laced neck, is typical of the style of soccer clothes worn in Europe at that time.

CHAMPIONS!
This game, called Championship Soccer, was made in 1983. It uses two of the classic components of many board games – dice and cards – to govern the movement of the ball around the field. A scoreboard and clock are also included.

QUICK CHANGE
These wooden blocks, with a different picture on each side, can be jumbled up to make a character. The shinpads and ball reflect the style of the time when the toy was made – 1895.

Memorabilia

SOCCER appeals to everyone, regardless of age or sex. The game can therefore be used to promote a wide range of items. Soccer-related advertising and product promotion is not a new phenomenon. In fact, companies were already latching on to the game's popularity in the early part of the 20th century. An understated style and original artwork predominated until the 1950s. This has been largely replaced by mass-produced items, heavily reliant on star players and wealthy teams.

1910 silver Vesta (match holder) advertising the mustard maker Colman's

Bank Top White Star

BAINES CARDS
These cards, produced in the early 20th century, were the forerunners of sticker albums and other collectables. They featured soccer and rugby league teams at the professional and amateur level and had advertisements on the reverse side.

Wednesday, now Sheffield Wednesday

Welsh national team

Chadderton, a nonleague team

Scottish club, Hearts

SPORTS CAN
By the 1930s, original artwork on a sports theme was often used as a decoration for everyday household items. This can features soccer on the lid and other sports, including cricket and hockey, around the outside.

Covered stands are rare in southern Europe.

FIFA logo for Italia '90

SOUVENIRS
Mementoes of the World Cup Finals do not stop at programs and tickets. There is great demand around the world for anything tied to the tournament, such as these erasers from Italia '90.

SOCCER FAN
This is a Spanish woman's fan from the mid 20th century, printed in Barcelona. It has a soccer image on one side and carries a promotional message on the reverse. Many commercial objects of this period were designed to be artistic as well as functional.

POSTER PAINTING
In this advertising card of the 1920s, an Italian liquor company has illustrated its product in a soccer scene, instead of putting a soccer image on the actual bottle.

VERMOUTH JACCOBINO

HEALTHY KICK
There is no magic ingredient in this drink, but the images would have appealed to soccer fans. The manufacturers knew that any association with soccer would improve sales.

FOOTBALL CUP SPECIAL QUALITY

This label comes from a fruity soft drink. It was marketed as an ideal refreshment for half-time.

CORONA BRAND FOOTBALL STOUT THOMAS & EVANS LTD PORTH.

This label implies that the drink will promote the strength that a soccer player enjoys.

Class B17 locomotive

Banks Johnstone Jennings England Best

TEAM TRAIN
In the early 1980s, the Hornby toy company of Liverpool, England, produced a series of these scale models of the London North Eastern Railway's locomotives, named after soccer teams. This one is called the *Manchester United*. Real trains are also sometimes named after teams.

Name plate

GASOLINE HEADS
The Cleveland Petrol company produced these miniatures of British international players in 1971. The set was given away free with gasoline sales.

The kicking leg is the second hand.

Pocket watch

Watch

Alarm clock

FULL TIME
This group includes a Swiss pocket watch made in Geneva around 1910, a British watch from the 1950s, and a more modern 1970s alarm clock. Design, materials, and, therefore, cost were dictated by whether the object was aimed at children or adults.

Chain

CHAIN MEDALS
Soccer items are often turned into jewelry and other personal effects. Four silver medals, struck in the 1920s, are attached to this chain. The silver locket and compass are from the 1880s.

Locket

Compass

More medals could be added to the chain.

OLYMPIC CLOCK
This German wooden clock may well have been made to commemorate the 1936 Berlin Olympics, where the soccer tournament was won by Italy, when they beat Austria 2–1 in the final. The figures at the top of the clock move on the hour.

The figure is the same on both halves.

CHOCOLATE
Melted chocolate would have been poured into this early 20th century brass mold and left to cool and set, producing a miniature chocolate soccer player with a ball at his feet. This item was made to appeal mainly to children, and the general soccer theme would have been enough to make it popular.

SOAP ON A ROPE
The Avon company produced this soap soccer ball to mark the 1966 World Cup Finals in England.

STRING ALONG
Made in the 1880s, this copper string holder prevents string from getting tangled. The string is pulled through a hole in the top.

The business of soccer

SOCCER IS BIG BUSINESS – fans attend games in large numbers, team products sell worldwide, and top players and managers earn incredibly large salaries. The people who started professionalism in the 1880s realized the financial possibilities of soccer, but for many decades the game carried on at much the same level. It provided inexpensive entertainment to the paying public and offered a decent living to players and managers. All that has changed now, as club owners and star players stretch soccer's money-making potential to the limit.

Gullit, pictured here in a preseason game, occasionally played for the teams he was managing as player-manager.

The emblem of the sponsoring local brewery

BILLY'S BRIBE
This shirt was worn by Welshman Billy Meredith, the greatest player of his era. He was one of several Manchester City, England, players who were banned from playing for a year in 1905. They allegedly tried to bribe the Aston Villa captain $15 to lose an important game. This was the first major scandal of British soccer.

GETTING SHIRTY
Replica shirts are a major source of income for professional teams like England's Manchester United and Spain's Real Madrid. Three or four designs are now available at one time, and new ones are brought out at regular intervals. Clubs produce hundreds of different products – from calenders to baby clothes; from candy to bicycles. These can be sold to fans all over the world, reducing the team's reliance on gate receipts.

MANAGEMENT STRESS
Managers are subjected to great stress in the modern game and have to accept that their every decision will be examined by the media. In most of the major leagues, the length of time allowed for a manager to produce a winning team can be measured in months rather than years. In 1999, Ruud Gullit was forced out of his job as manager of England's Newcastle United after just a few unsuccessful months.

Even shinpads, worn under the socks, are marked with the name of the manufacturer.

SHIRT AD
In the 1970s, businesses began to pay for the right to advertise on team uniforms. Within a few years, even nonleague teams had some income from this source. Pictured here are players from Real Madrid, Spain, and Inter Milan, Italy, sporting their sponsor's logos.

Strikers, such as Papin, fetch the highest prices.

Papin's shirt advertises a French supermarket.

MILLION-DOLLAR MAN

Jean-Pierre Papin became the first $15 million player, when he moved from Marseille, France, to AC Milan, Italy, in 1992. Since then, salaries have continued to rocket, with Italian Christian Vieri joining Inter Milan from Lazio, Italy, for $45 million in 1999. Players today are eager to move regularly because of the signing fees they receive. Teams often make record signings, even when they are heavily in debt.

Foreign players, including Di Matteo, are in the majority at Chelsea, England

ALL ABROAD!

Political and legal changes have made it easy for soccer players to move abroad and play for foreign clubs. European Union residents can now play in any member state. Roberto di Matteo was one of the first Italians to transfer to an English club in 1996. Since then, a ruling has established that a club does not have to pay for a player whose contract has expired.

GROUND FORCE

Advertising in and around soccer fields was allowed long before shirt sponsorship. In the 1950s, it featured mainly local firms, but now larger multinational companies exploit the exposure provided by television coverage. Some billboards rotate, to catch the eye of the watching public and allow more advertisers to use limited space. In some competitions, such as the European Champion's League, the same products are advertised at every game in the tournament.

Patch showing AC Milan's club logo

World Club Cup

Brand logos are clearly visible on boots.

MEDIA MOGULS

AC Milan is one of the many teams with links to big business. Italian media mogul Silvio Berlusconi bought the club at a time when television coverage of the game was increasing. He was able to maximize commercial opportunities and attract star players from abroad.

WORLD CHAMPIONS

The first World Club Cup was contested by Real Madrid and Penarol, Uruguay, in 1960. It has been treated as an exhibition match and held in Tokyo, Japan, since 1980. The 21st century, however, will see it expand into a tournament for the champion club from each continent. This will be attractive to TV audiences and bring in money through advertising, but will place further demands on players and managers.

Index

A

AC Milan, 16, 59
Accrington Stanley, 24, 38
advantage rule, 12
advertising, 56, 58, 59
Africa, 11
African Nations Cup, 39, 43, 53
Ajax, 40
amateurism, 10, 14
American football, 27
Argentina, 23, 41, 51, 53
assistant referees, 12, 13, 14, 15
autograph books, 42

B

badges, 45, 48
bagatelle, 54
Baggio, Roberto, 19
ball control, 18
ball pumps, 27
ball repair kit, 27
Banks, Gordon, 34
Barcelona, 41, 46
Batistuta, Gabriel, 19
Bayern Munich, 41, 52
Beckenbauer, Franz, 37, 41
Beckham, David, 19
bells, 43
belts, 32
Benfica, 40, 52
Berlusconi, Silvio, 59
bicycle kick, 19
Bierhoff, Oliver, 18
bladders, 26, 27
bookings, 15
books, 9, 15
bootlaces, 29
Brazil, 43, 46, 49, 50, 53
bribery, 58
British Ladies Club, 11, 40
business, 58, 59

C

calcio, 8, 27
caps, 38
card games, 55
Carey, John, 39
Carlos, Roberto, 18
Chapman, Herbert, 22
Charlton, Bobby, 34
Chile, 50
China, 8
clocks, 57
clockwork toys, 55
clothes:
  soccer uniforms, 30-31
  goalkeeper's, 20, 21
  referee's, 14, 15
cleats, 29
clubs, 40-41
collecting, 42
commercialism, 50, 58, 59

competitions, 10, 52
computer games, 54
Copa America, 52, 53
Copa Libertadores, 41
Corinthians, 10, 28
corner flags, 13
corner kicks, 12, 19
crosses, 19
crowd control, 45
Cruyff, Johann, 34, 40
cups, 52, 53

D

defenders, 18, 23
Di Matteo, Roberto, 59
Di Stefano, Alfredo, 37, 41
doctors, 25
double, League and Cup, 38
drainage, 17
dribbling, 19, 26

E

Egypt, 11, 53
England, 8, 10, 41
entertainment, pre-match, 44
European Cup, 40, 41, 52, 53
Eusebio, 35
exhibition matches, 10

F

FA Cup, 10, 13, 44
  trophy, 53
face painting, 43
fans, see supporters
FIFA, 11, 14, 15, 23, 48, 50
Finney, Tom, 39
fitness, 24
floodlights, 46
Football Association, 10
  badges, 45
Football League, 10
foreign players, 59
fouls, 12, 13
France, 11, 18, 22, 40, 47, 51
free kicks, 12
Fry, C. B., 10, 43

G

Garrincha, 35, 49
Gascoigne, Paul, 25
Germany, 41
gifts, 38
gloves, 20, 33
goalkeeper, 13, 20, 21
goal kicks, 12, 21
goal nets, 13
goal posts, 12
groundstaff, 16, 17
Gullit, Ruud, 58

H

hamstring injuries, 25
Harrow school, 8

hats, 33
heading, 18, 26
Heysel Stadium disaster, 52
Hillsborough disaster, 46
Holland, 22, 30, 40
Home Internationals, 39
Honeyball, Netty, 40
Hungary, 38

I

Independiente, 41
injuries, 23, 24, 25
international, first, 10
Ireland, 20
Italy, 8, 24, 40

J

Jack Kent Cooke Stadium, 51
James, Alex, 31, 38
Japan, 9
jerseys, 30
Juventus, 40

K

Kelly, Alan, 20
kemari, 9
Kempes, Mario, 51
Kick game, 55
kick-off, 12, 13
Kinnaird, Lord, 10
Kirke Smith, Arnold, 10
Kopa, Raymond, 36
Leonidas, 19
Lofthouse, Nat, 13

M

McCracken, William, 23
managers, 22, 58
Manchester United, 13, 21, 34, 41
Maracana Stadium, Rio de Janeiro, 46, 48
Maradona, Diego, 35
Marseilles, 40
mascots, World Cup, 48, 50
match day, 44, 45
Matthews, Stanley, 36
Meazza, Guiseppe, 35
medals, 38, 57
medicine bags, 25
medicine balls, 24
merchandise, 39, 42, 51, 54, 56, 57, 58
Meredith, Billy, 58
midfielders, 18, 22
Milla, Roger, 34
money-boxes, 42
Muller, Gerd, 34, 41
Munich air crash, 34, 41

N

narrowing the angle, 21
Newcastle United, 30
Norway, 23
Nou Camp stadium, Barcelona, 46

O

offside rule, 12, 13, 23
offside trap, 23
Olympic Games, 52, 57
Orkney Isles, 27
Overmars, Marc, 30

P

pallone, 27
Papin, Jean-Pierre, 16, 59
passing, 18
Pele, 37, 48, 49
penalties, 12, 13
pencil cases, 42
physiotherapists, 24, 25
pitch, 13, 16, 17
  artificial, 17
plaques, 38
Platini, Michel, 37
players, 34, 37
police, 45
Portugal, 40
Pozzo, Vittorio, 24
private schools, 8, 10, 28, 39
professional fouls, 12
professionalism, 10, 14, 18, 58
programs, 44, 49, 52
private schools, 8, 10, 28, 39
punching the ball, 20
Puskas, Ferenc, 37, 41

R

rattles, 43
Ravelli, Thomas, 38
Real Madrid, 41, 52, 59
red and yellow cards, 14
referees, 14, 15
Rimet, Jules, 40, 49
Ronaldo, 19, 51
Rose Bowl, 52
rules, 12-13, 20, 30

S

San Siro stadium, Milan, 17
Schmeichel, Peter, 21
Scotland, 10
set-pieces, 23
shinpads, 32, 33, 58
shirts, 20, 30
  goalkeepers', 20
shooting, 19
shoes, 28, 29
shorts, 31
shouting, 18, 21
Shrove Tuesday games, 8
signing fees, 59
skills, 18, 19
soccer balls, 26, 27
soccer cards, 56
socks, 31
souvenirs, 56
sponges, 24
sponsorship, 58, 59
Stade de France, St Denis, 47
stadiums, 17, 46, 47

O

advertising in, 59
stands, 17, 47
street soccer, 9, 16, 27
stretchers, 24
strikers, 18
Suarez, Luis, 36
substitutions, 13, 14, 23, 25
supporters, 42, 43, 44, 58
sweeper system, 22

T

tackling, 18
tactics, 22, 23
team formations, 22
terraces, 47
Three Lions motif, 10, 45
throwing out, 21
Thuram, Lilian, 18, 51
tickets, 44
total football, 22
tournaments, 52, 53
toys, 54, 55, 57
trainers, 39
training, 18, 20, 24
Trench Football game, 54
trophies, 52, 53
  World Cup, 49, 50
tunnel, 46

U

UEFA Cup, 53
umpires, 14
Uruguay, 48, 53
USA, 11, 45, 51, 52

V

Van Basten, Marco, 36

W

warm-up, 24
watches, 15, 57
Wembley Stadium, 46
whistle, referee's, 14
Widdowson, Samuel, 32
wing-backs, 22
wingers, 22
women's football, 11, 40
  clothing, 31, 33
Women's World Cup, 11, 52
  trophy, 52
World Club Cup, 59
World Cup, 40, 48, 51, 56
  balls, 26
  draw, 51
  first, 11, 48 47
  medals, 38, 39
  opening ceremony, 44
  referees, 15
  staging of, 48, 51
  trophies, 49, 51
  winners, 48
World Cup Willie, 50
World Wars, 54, 39, 43

Y

Yashin, Lev, 36

Z

Zagalo, Mario, 49
Zidane, Zinedine, 18

Acknowledgments

Dorling Kindersley would like to thank:
Hugh Hornby, Rob Pratten, and Lynsey Jones at the Football Museum for their help and patience.

Chris Bernstein for the index

The publishers would also like to thank the following for their kind permission to reproduce their photographs:

a=above; c=center; b=below; l=left; r=right; t=top; f=far; n=near;

Action Plus: 58bl; Glyn Kirk 15l, 18tr, 18cl, 18br, 19tl, 23cr, 44br, 51bl, 58clb; Matthew Clarke 19c; Neil Tingle 12br.
Allsport: 34cl, 34br, 35tl, 35c; Ben Radford 58cr; Christopher Guibbaud 59tl; Claudio Villa 18bl; Clive Brunskill 16bl; David Cannon 19c, 53cr; David Leah 53c; Don Morley 18br; Hulton Getty 36bl; Jed Jacbsohn 52c; Michael Cooper 59c; Michael King 36-7bc; Scott R Indermaur 45tl; Vincent Laforet 52br.
Bryan Horsnell: 44cl, 44cfl, 44cnl.
Colorsport: 12tr, 13tr, 21r, 23br, 29tr, 30tr, 34bl, 41br, 46-7b, 59tr; Jerome Provost 41bc; Olympia 36br, 37tr.
Corbis UK Ltd: S Carmona 46clb.

Empics Ltd: 34tnr; Don Morley 37tr; Michael Steele 43bl, 43br; Neale Simpson 40cl; Peter Robinson 36bc, 49l, 59br; Tony Marshall 19bl; Topham Picturepoint 36bc, 37tl; Witters 34tr.
Hulton Getty: 19bl, 35cr, 35bl, 36tl.
Mark Leech: 45bl.
Popperfoto: 53cl.
Sporting Pictures (uk) Ltd: 4cr, 24cl, 25tl, 25tr, 33br, 38bl, 46cl.

Jacket
Allsport: front cl; Graham Chadwick back bl; Gary M Prior back cl; Ben Radford front cr.
Bryan Horsnell: back cb, back cbl, back tc, back cbr, front tc.
Colorsport: back br, back cla.
Mary Evans Picture Library: spine, front tcr.
The Robert Opie Collection: back tfl, back tfl, front tr.

DK EYEWITNESS BOOKS

SUBJECTS

HISTORY

AFRICA

ANCIENT CHINA

ARMS & ARMOR

BATTLE

CASTLE

COWBOY

EXPLORER

KNIGHT

MEDIEVAL LIFE

MYTHOLOGY

NORTH AMERICAN INDIAN

PIRATE

PRESIDENTS

RUSSIA

SHIPWRECK

TITANIC

VIKING

WITCHES & MAGIC-MAKERS

ANCIENT WORLDS

ANCIENT EGYPT

ANCIENT GREECE

ANCIENT ROME

AZTEC, INCA & MAYA

BIBLE LANDS

MUMMY

PYRAMID

THE BEGINNINGS OF LIFE

ARCHEOLOGY

DINOSAUR

EARLY HUMANS

PREHISTORIC LIFE

THE ARTS

BOOK

COSTUME

DANCE

FILM

MUSIC

TECHNOLOGY

BOAT

CAR

FLYING MACHINE

FUTURE

INVENTION

SPACE EXPLORATION

TRAIN

PAINTING

GOYA

IMPRESSIONISM

LEONARDO & HIS TIMES

MANET

MONET

PERSPECTIVE

RENAISSANCE

VAN GOGH

WATERCOLOR

SCIENCE

ASTRONOMY

CHEMISTRY

EARTH

ECOLOGY

ELECTRICITY

ELECTRONICS

ENERGY

EVOLUTION

FORCE & MOTION

HUMAN BODY

LIFE

LIGHT

MATTER

MEDICINE

SKELETON

TECHNOLOGY

TIME & SPACE

SPORT

BASEBALL

FOOTBALL

OLYMPICS

SOCCER

SPORTS

ANIMALS

AMPHIBIAN

BIRD

BUTTERFLY & MOTH

CAT

DOG

EAGLE &
BIRDS OF PREY

ELEPHANT

FISH

GORILLA,
MONKEY & APE

HORSE

INSECT

MAMMAL

REPTILE

SHARK

WHALE

HABITATS

ARCTIC & ANTARCTIC

DESERT

JUNGLE

OCEAN

POND & RIVER

SEASHORE

THE EARTH

CRYSTAL & GEM

FOSSIL

HURRICANE &
TORNADO

PLANT

ROCKS & MINERALS

SHELL

TREE

VOLCANO &
EARTHQUAKE

WEATHER

THE WORLD AROUND US

BUILDING

CRIME & DETECTION

FARM

FLAG

MEDIA &
COMMUNICATIONS

MONEY

RELIGION

SPY

Future updates and editions will be available online at www.dk.com

EYEWITNESS BOOKS

A–Z

AFRICA 61
AMPHIBIAN 41
ANCIENT CHINA 55
ANCIENT EGYPT 23
ANCIENT GREECE 37
ANCIENT ROME 24
ARCHEOLOGY 56
ARCTIC & ANTARCTIC 57
ARMS & ARMOR 4
ASTRONOMY 82
AZTEC, INCA & MAYA 47

BASEBALL 110
BATTLE 63
BIBLE LANDS 30
BIRD 1
BOAT 36
BOOK 48
BUILDING 58
BUTTERFLY & MOTH 7

CAR 21
CASTLE 49
CAT 29
CHEMISTRY 79
COSTUME 35
COWBOY 45
CRIME & DETECTION 73
CRYSTAL & GEM 25

DANCE 99
DESERT 51
DINOSAUR 13
DOG 32

EAGLE & BIRDS OF PREY 69
EARLY HUMANS 10
EARTH 83
ECOLOGY 86
ELECTRICITY 77
ELECTRONICS 90
ELEPHANT 42
ENERGY 76

EVOLUTION 85
EXPLORER 31

FARM 66
FILM 34
FISH 20
FLAG 16
FLYING MACHINE 22
FOOTBALL 106
FORCE & MOTION 78
FOSSIL 19
FUTURE 100

GORILLA, MONKEY
& APE 64
GOYA 93

HORSE 33
HUMAN BODY 87
HURRICANE &
TORNADO 107

IMPRESSIONISM 92
INSECT 17
INVENTION 27

JUNGLE 54

KNIGHT 43

LEONARDO &
HIS TIMES 102
LIFE 84
LIGHT 75

MAMMAL 11
MANET 94
MATTER 80
MEDIA &
COMMUNICATIONS 104
MEDICINE 88
MEDIEVAL LIFE 65
MONET 95
MONEY 18
MUMMY 44
MUSIC 12
MYTHOLOGY 101

NORTH AMERICAN
INDIAN 60

OCEAN 62
OLYMPICS 103

PERSPECTIVE 98
PIRATE 59
PLANT 14
POND & RIVER 6
PREHISTORIC LIFE 52
PRESIDENTS 109
PYRAMID 53

RELIGION 68
RENAISSANCE 91
REPTILE 26
ROCKS & MINERALS 2
RUSSIA 74

SEASHORE 15
SHARK 40
SHELL 9
SHIPWRECK 72
SKELETON 3
SOCCER 108
SPACE EXPLORATION 71
SPORTS 8
SPY 67

TECHNOLOGY 89
TIME & SPACE 81
TITANIC 105
TRAIN 39
TREE 5

VAN GOGH 96
VIKING 50
VOLCANO &
EARTHQUAKE 38

WATERCOLOR 97
WEATHER 28
WHALE 46
WITCHES &
MAGIC-MAKERS 70

DK EYEWITNESS BOOKS

1–110

1 BIRD
2 ROCKS & MINERALS
3 SKELETON
4 ARMS AND ARMOR
5 TREE
6 POND & RIVER
7 BUTTERFLY & MOTH
8 SPORTS
9 SHELL
10 EARLY HUMANS

11 MAMMAL
12 MUSIC
13 DINOSAUR
14 PLANT
15 SEASHORE
16 FLAG
17 INSECT
18 MONEY
19 FOSSIL
20 FISH

21 CAR
22 FLYING MACHINE
23 ANCIENT EGYPT
24 ANCIENT ROME
25 CRYSTAL & GEM
26 REPTILE
27 INVENTION
28 WEATHER
29 CAT
30 BIBLE LANDS

31 EXPLORER
32 DOG
33 HORSE
34 FILM
35 COSTUME
36 BOAT
37 ANCIENT GREECE
38 VOLCANO &
   EARTHQUAKE

39 TRAIN
40 SHARK
41 AMPHIBIAN
42 ELEPHANT
43 KNIGHT
44 MUMMY
45 COWBOY
46 WHALE
47 AZTEC, INCA & MAYA
48 BOOK
49 CASTLE
50 VIKING

51 DESERT
52 PREHISTORIC LIFE
53 PYRAMID
54 JUNGLE
55 ANCIENT CHINA
56 ARCHEOLOGY
57 ARCTIC & ANTARCTIC
58 BUILDING
59 PIRATE
60 NORTH AMERICAN
   INDIAN

61 AFRICA
62 OCEAN
63 BATTLE
64 GORILLA, MONKEY
   & APE
65 MEDIEVAL LIFE
66 FARM
67 SPY
68 RELIGION
69 EAGLE & BIRDS OF PREY
70 WITCHES &
   MAGIC-MAKERS

71 SPACE EXPLORATION
72 SHIPWRECK
73 CRIME & DETECTION
74 RUSSIA

75 LIGHT
76 ENERGY
77 ELECTRICITY
78 FORCE & MOTION
79 CHEMISTRY
80 MATTER

81 TIME & SPACE
82 ASTRONOMY
83 EARTH
84 LIFE
85 EVOLUTION
86 ECOLOGY
87 HUMAN BODY
88 MEDICINE
89 TECHNOLOGY
90 ELECTRONICS

91 RENAISSANCE
92 IMPRESSIONISM
93 GOYA
94 MANET
95 MONET
96 VAN GOGH
97 WATERCOLOR
98 PERSPECTIVE
99 DANCE
100 FUTURE

101 MYTHOLOGY
102 LEONARDO & HIS TIMES
103 OLYMPICS
104 MEDIA &
   COMMUNICATIONS
105 TITANIC
106 FOOTBALL
107 HURRICANE & TORNADO
108 SOCCER
109 PRESIDENTS
110 BASEBALL

Future updates and editions will be available online at www.dk.com